Siegel's
WILLS & TRUSTS

Essay and Multiple-Choice Questions and Answers

Brian N. Siegel
J.D., Columbia Law School

and

Lazar Emanuel
J.D., Harvard Law School

Aspen Law & Business
Legal Education Division
New York   Gaithersburg

D1510683

Printed in the United States of America.

ISBN 0-7355-2737-7

1 2 3 4 5 6 7 8 9 0

This book is intended as a general review of a legal subject. It is not intended as a source of advice for the solution of legal matters or problems. For advice on legal matters, the reader should consult an attorney.

About Aspen Law & Business
Legal Education Division

Aspen Law & Business is proud to welcome Emanuel Publishing Corporation's highly successful study aids to its list of law school publications. As part of the Aspen family, Steve and Lazar Emanuel will continue their work on these popular titles, widely purchased by students for more than a quarter century. With the addition of the Emanuel titles, Aspen now offers the most comprehensive selection of outstanding publications for the discerning law student.

ASPEN LAW & BUSINESS
A Division of Aspen Publishers, Inc.
A Wolters Kluwer Company
www.aspenpublishers.com

About the Authors

Professor Brian N. Siegel received his *Juris Doctorate* from Columbia Law School, where he was designated a Harlan Fiske Stone Scholar for academic excellence. He is the author of *How to Succeed in Law School* and numerous works pertaining to preparation for the California Bar examination. Professor Siegel has taught as a member of the adjunct faculty at Pepperdine School of Law and Whittier College School of Law, as well as for the UCLA Extension Program.

Lazar Emanuel is a graduate of Harvard Law School. In 1950, he became a founding partner of the New York law firm now known as Cowan, Liebowitz & Latman. From 1960 through 1971, he was president of Communications Industries Corp., multiple licensee of radio and television stations in the Northeast. He has edited many of the publications in the Professor Series of study aids and in the Siegel's Series. He is publisher of The New York Professional Responsibility Report and author of *Latin For Lawyers*.

Acknowledgment

The authors gratefully acknowledge the assistance of the California Committee of Bar Examiners, which provided access to questions upon which many of the questions in this book are based.

Introduction

Although your grades are a significant factor in obtaining a summer internship or permanent position at a law firm, no formalized preparation for finals is offered at most law schools. Students, for the most part, are expected to fend for themselves in learning the exam-taking process. Ironically, law school exams ordinarily bear little correspondence to the teaching methods used by professors during the school year. The professors require you to spend most of your time briefing cases. Although many claim this is "great preparation" for issue-spotting on exams, it really isn't. Because you focus on one principle of law at a time, you don't get practice in relating one issue to another or in developing a picture of the entire course. When exams finally come, you're forced to make an abrupt 180-degree turn. Suddenly, you are asked to recognize, define and discuss a variety of issues buried within a single multi-issue fact pattern. In most schools, you are then asked to select among a number of possible answers, all of which look inviting but only one of which is right.

Your comprehensive course outline, which you've created so diligently and with such pain, means little if you're unable to apply its contents on your final exams. There is a vast difference between reading opinions in which the legal principles are clearly stated, and applying those same principles to hypothetical exams and multiple choice questions.

The purpose of this book is to help you bridge the gap between memorizing a rule of law and **understanding how to use it** in the context of an exam. After an initial overview describing the exam writing process, you will be presented with a large number of hypotheticals which test your ability to write analytical essays and to pick the right answers to multiple-choice questions. **Do them — all of them!** Then review the suggested answers which follow. You'll find that the key to superior grades lies in applying your knowledge through questions and answers, not through rote memory.

GOOD LUCK !

Table of Contents

Essay Exam Answers

Multiple Choice Questions

Multiple Choice Answers

Tables and Index

Preparing Effectively for Essay Examinations[1]

To achieve superior scores on essay exams, a student must (i) learn and understand "blackletter" principles and rules of law for each subject, and (ii) analyze how those principles of law arise within a test fact pattern. One of the most common misconceptions about law school is that you must memorize each word on every page of your casebooks or outlines to do well on exams. The reality is that you can commit an entire casebook to memory and still do poorly on an exam. Reviewing hundreds of student answers has shown us that most students can recite the rules. The ones who do *best* on exams understand how problems (issues) stem from the rules which they have memorized and how to communicate their analysis of these issues to the grader. The following pages cover what you need to know to achieve superior scores on your law school essay exams.

The "ERC" Process

To study effectively for law school exams you must be able to *"ERC"* (*E*lementize, *R*ecognize, and *C*onceptualize) each legal principle listed in the table of contents of your casebooks and course outlines. *Elementizing* means reducing the legal theories and rules you learn, down to a concise, straightforward statement of their essential elements. Without a knowledge of these precise elements, it is not possible to anticipate all of the potential issues which can arise under them.

For example, if you are asked, "what is self-defense?", it is *not* sufficient to say, "self-defense is permitted when, if someone is about to hit you, you can prevent him from doing it." This layperson description would leave a grader wondering if you had actually attended law school. An accurate elementization of the self-defense principle would be something like this: "Where one reasonably believes she is in imminent danger of an offensive touching, she may assert whatever force she reasonably believes necessary under the circumstances to prevent the offensive touching from occurring." This formulation correctly shows that there are four separate, distinct elements which must be satisfied for this defense to be successfully asserted: (i) the actor must have a *reasonable belief* that (ii) the touching which she seeks to prevent is *offensive*, (iii) the offensive touching is *imminent*, and (iv) the actor must use no greater force than she *reasonably*

---

1. To illustrate the principles of effective exam preparation, we have used examples from Torts and Constitutional Law. However, these principles apply to all subjects. One of the most difficult tasks faced by law students is learning how to apply principles from one area of the law to another. We leave it to you, the reader, to think of comparable examples for the subject-matter of this book.

believes is necessary under the circumstances to prevent the offensive touching from occurring.

Recognizing means perceiving or anticipating which words within a legal principle are likely to be the source of issues, and how those issues are likely to arise within a hypothetical fact pattern. With respect to the self-defense concept, there are four ***potential*** issues. Did the actor reasonably believe that the person against whom the defense is being asserted was about to make an offensive contact upon her? Was the contact imminent? Would the contact have been offensive? Did the actor use only such force as she reasonably believed was necessary to prevent the imminent, offensive touching?

Conceptualizing means imagining situations in which the elements of a rule of law have given rise to factual issues. ***Unless a student can illustrate to herself an application of each element of a rule of law, she does not truly understand the legal principles behind the rule!*** In our opinion, the inability to conjure up hypothetical problems involving particular rules of law foretells a likelihood that issues involving those rules will be missed on an exam. It is therefore ***crucial*** to (i) ***recognize*** that issues result from the interaction of facts with the appropriate words defining a rule of law; and ii) develop the ability to ***conceptualize*** fact patterns involving each of the words contained in the rule.

For example, an illustration of the "reasonable belief" portion of the self-defense principle in tort law might be the following:

> One evening, A and B had an argument at a bar. A screamed at B, "I'm going to get a knife and stab you!" A then ran out of the bar. B, who was armed with a concealed pistol, left the bar about 15 minutes later. As B was walking home, he suddenly heard running footsteps coming up from behind him. B drew his pistol, turned and shot the person advancing toward him (who was only about ten feet away when the shooting occurred). When B walked over to his victim, he recognized that the person he had killed was not A (but was instead another individual who had simply decided to take an evening jog). There would certainly be an issue whether B had a reasonable belief that the person who was running behind him was A. In the subsequent wrongful-death action, the victim's estate would certainly contend that the earlier threat by A was not enough to give B a reasonable belief that the person running behind him was A. B could certainly contend in rebuttal that given the prior altercation at the bar, A's threat, the darkness, and the fact that the incident occurred within a time frame soon after A's threat, his belief that A was about to attack him was "reasonable."

An illustration of how use of the word "imminent" might generate an issue is the following:

> X and Y had been feuding for some time. One afternoon, X suddenly attacked Y with a hunting knife. However, Y was able to wrest the knife away From X.

> At that point X retreated about four feet away from Y and screamed: "You were lucky this time, but next time I'll have a gun and you'll be finished." Y, having good reason to believe that X would subsequently carry out his threats (after all, X had just attempted to kill Y), immediately thrust the knife into X's chest, killing him. While Y certainly had a reasonable belief that X would attempt to kill him the *next time* the two met, Y would probably *not* be able to successfully assert the self-defense privilege since the "imminency" element was absent.

A fact pattern illustrating the actor's right to use only that force which is reasonably necessary under the circumstances might be the following:

> D rolled up a newspaper and was about to strike E on the shoulder with it. As D pulled back his arm for the purpose of delivering the blow, E drew a knife and plunged it into D's chest. While E had every reason to believe that D was about to deliver an offensive impact on him, E probably could not successfully assert the self-defense privilege because the force he utilized in response was greater than reasonably necessary under the circumstances to prevent the impact. E could simply have deflected D's prospective blow or punched D away. The use of a knife constituted a degree of force by E which was *not* reasonable, given the minor injury which he would have suffered from the newspaper's impact.

"Mental gymnastics" such as these must be played with every element of every rule you learn.

Issue-Spotting

One of the keys to doing well on an essay examination is issue-spotting. In fact, issue spotting is ***the*** most important skill you will learn in law school. If you recognize all of the legal issues, you can always find an applicable rule of law (if there is any) by researching the issues. However, if you fail to perceive an issue, you may very well misadvise your client about the likelihood of success or failure. It is important to remember that (1) an issue is a question to be decided by the judge or jury; and (2) a question is "in issue" when it can be disputed or argued about at trial. The bottom line is that ***if you don't spot an issue, you can't discuss it.***

The key to issue-spotting is to approach a problem in the same way as an attorney would. Let's assume you're a lawyer and someone enters your office with a legal problem. He will recite the facts to you and give you any documents that may be pertinent. He will then want to know if he can sue (or be sued, if your client seeks to avoid liability). To answer your client's question intelligently, you will have to decide the following: (1) what theories can possibly be asserted by your client; (2) what defense or defenses can possibly be raised to these theories; (3) what issues may arise if these theories and defenses are asserted; (4) what arguments can each side make to persuade the factfinder to resolve the issue in his favor; and (5) finally, what will the *likely* outcome of each issue be. *All the issues which can possibly arise at trial should be discussed in your answer.*

How to Discuss an Issue

Keep in mind that *rules of law are the guides to issues* (*i.e.*, an issue arises where there is a question whether the facts do, or do not, satisfy an element of a rule); a rule of law *cannot dispose of an issue* unless the rule can reasonably be *applied to the facts.*

A good way to learn how to discuss an issue is to start with the following mini-hypothetical and the two student responses which follow it.

Mini-Hypothetical

A and B were involved in making a movie which was being filmed at a bar. The script called for A to appear to throw a bottle (which was actually a rubber prop) at B. The fluorescent lighting at the bar had been altered, the subdued blue lights being replaced with rather bright white lights. The cameraperson had stationed herself just to the left of the swinging doors which served as the main entrance to the bar. As the scene was unfolding, C, a regular patron of the bar, unwittingly walked into it. The guard who was stationed immediately out-side the bar, had momentarily left his post to visit the restroom. As C pushed the barroom doors inward, the left door panel knocked the camera to the ground with a resounding crash. The first (and only) thing which C saw, how-ever, was A (who was about 5 feet from C) getting ready to throw the bottle at B, who was at the other end of the bar (about 15 feet from A). Without hesita-tion, C pushed A to the ground and punched him in the face. Plastic surgery was required to restore A's profile to its Hollywood-handsome pre-altercation form.

Discuss A's right against C.

Pertinent Principles of Law:

1. Under the rule defining the prevention-of-crime privilege, if one sees that someone is about to commit what she reasonably believes to be a felony or misdemeanor involving a breach of the peace, she may exercise whatever degree of force is reasonably necessary under the circumstances to prevent that person from committing the crime.

2. Under the defense-of-others privilege, where one reasonably believes that someone is about to cause an offensive contact upon a third party, she may use whatever force is reasonably necessary under the circumstances to prevent the contact. Some jurisdictions, however, limit this privilege to situations in which

the actor and the third party are related.

First Student Answer

"Did C commit an assault and battery upon A?

"An assault occurs where the defendant intentionally causes the plaintiff to be reasonably in apprehension of an imminent, offensive touching. The facts state that C punched A to the ground. Thus, a battery would have occurred at this point. We are also told that C punched A in the face. It is reasonable to assume that A saw the punch being thrown at him, and therefore A felt in imminent danger of an offensive touching. Based upon the facts, C is liable for an assault and battery upon A.

"Were C's actions justifiable under the defense-of-others privilege?

"C could successfully assert the defense of others and prevention of crime privileges. When C opened the bar doors, A appeared to be throwing the bottle at B. Although the "bottle" was actually a prop, C had no way of knowing this fact. Also, it was necessary for C to punch A in the face to assure that A could not get back up, retrieve the bottle, and again throw it at B. While the plastic surgery required by A is unfortunate, C could not be successfully charged with assault and battery."

Second Student Answer

"Assault and Battery:

"C committed an assault (causing A to be reasonably in apprehension of an imminent, offensive contact) when A saw C's punch about to hit him, and battery (causing an offensive contact upon A) when he (i) C knocked A to the ground, and (ii) C punched A.

"Defense-of-Others/Prevention-of-Crime Defenses:

"C would undoubtedly assert the privileges of defense-of-others (where defendant reasonably believed the plaintiff was about to make an offensive contact upon a third party, he was entitled to use whatever force was reasonably necessary to prevent the contact); and prevention-of-crime defense (where one reasonably believes another is about to commit a felony or misdemeanor involving a breach of the peace, he may exercise whatever force is reasonably necessary to prevent that person from committing a crime).

"A could contend that C was not reasonable in believing that A was about to cause harm to B because the enhanced lighting at the bar and camera crash should have indicated to C, a regular customer, that a movie was being filmed. However, C could probably successfully contend in rebuttal that his belief was reasonable in light of the facts that (i) he had not seen the camera when he attacked A, and (ii) instantaneous action was required (he did not have time to notice the enhanced lighting around the bar).

"A might also contend that the justification was forfeited because the degree of force used by C was not reasonable, since C did not have to punch A in the face after A had already been pushed to the ground (*i.e.*, the danger to B was no longer present). However, C could argue in rebuttal that it was necessary to knock out A (an individual with apparently violent propensities) while the opportunity existed, rather than risk a drawn-out scuffle in which A might prevail. The facts do not indicate how big A and C were; but assuming C was not significantly larger than A, C's contention will probably be successful. If, however, C was significantly larger than A, the punch may have been excessive (since C could presumably have simply held A down)."

Critique

Let's examine the First Student Answer first. It mistakenly phrases as an "issue" the assault and battery committed by C upon A. While the actions creating these torts must be mentioned in the facts to provide a foundation for a discussion of the applicable privileges, there was no need to discuss them further because they were not the issue the examiners were testing for.

The structure of the initial paragraph of First Student Answer is also incorrect. After an assault is defined in the first sentence, the second sentence abruptly describes the facts necessary to constitute the commission of a battery. The third sentence then sets forth the elements of a battery. The fourth sentence completes the discussion of assault by describing the facts pertaining to that tort. The two-sentence break between the original mention of assault and the facts which constitute this tort is confusing; the facts which call for the application of a rule should be mentioned *immediately* after the rule is stated.

A more serious error, however, occurs in the second paragraph of the First Student Answer. While there is an allusion to the correct principle of law (prevention of crime), the *rule is not defined*. As a consequence, the grader can only guess why the student thinks the facts set forth in the subsequent sentences are significant. A grader reading this answer could not be certain that the student recognized that the issues revolved around the *reasonable belief* and *necessary force* elements of the prevention-of-crime privilege. Superior exam-writing requires that the pertinent facts be *tied* directly and clearly to the operative rule.

The Second Student Answer is very much better than the First Answer. It disposes of C's assault and battery upon A in a few words (yet tells the grader that the writer knows these torts are present). More importantly, the grader can easily see the issues which would arise if the prevention-of crime-privilege were asserted (*i.e.*, "whether C's belief that A was about to commit a crime against B was reasonable" and "whether C used unnecessary force in punching A after A had been knocked to the ground"). Finally, it also utilizes all the facts by indicating how each attorney would assert those facts which are most advantageous to her client.

Structuring Your Answer

Graders will give high marks to a clearly-written, well-structured answer. Each issue you discuss should follow a specific and consistent structure which a grader can easily follow.

The Second Student Answer above basically utilizes the *I-R-A-A-O format* with respect to each issue. In this format, the *"I"* stands for the word *"Issue;"* the *"R"* for *"Rule of law"*; the initial *"A"* for the words *"one side's Argument"*; the second *"A"* for *"the other party's rebuttal Argument"*; and the *"O"* for your *"Opinion as to how the issue would be resolved."* The *I-R-A-A-O* format emphasizes the importance of (1) discussing *both* sides of an issue, and (2) communicating to the grader that when an issue arises, an attorney can only advise her client as to the *probable* decision on that issue.

A somewhat different format for analyzing each issue is the *I-R-A-C format*. Here, the *"I"* stands for *"Issue"*; the *"R"* for *"Rule of law"*; the *"A"* for *"Application of the facts to the rule of law"*; and the *"C"* for *"Conclusion."* *I-R-A-C* is a legitimate approach to the discussion of a particular issue, within the time constraints imposed by the question. The *I-R-A-C format* must be applied to each issue; it is not the solution to an entire exam answer. If there are six issues in a question, for example, you should offer six separate, independent *I-R-A-C* analyses.

We believe that the *I-R-A-C* approach is preferable to the *I-R-A-A-O* formula. However, either can be used to analyze and organize essay exam answers. Whatever format you choose, however, you should be consistent throughout the exam and remember the following rules:

First, *analyze all of the relevant facts*. Facts have significance in a particular case *only as they come under the applicable rules of law*. The facts presented must be analyzed and examined to see if they do or do not satisfy one element or another of the applicable rules, and the essential facts and rules must be stated and argued in your analysis.

Second, you must communicate to the grader the ***precise rule of law*** controlling the facts. In their eagerness to commence their arguments, students sometimes fail to state the applicable rule of law first. Remember, the ***"R"*** in either format stands for "Rule of Law." Defining the rule of law ***before*** an analysis of the facts is essential in order to allow the grader to follow your reasoning.

Third, it is important to treat ***each side of an issue with equal detail.*** If a hypothetical describes how an elderly man was killed when he ventured upon the land of a huge power company to obtain a better view of a nuclear reactor, your sympathies might understandably fall on the side of the old man. The grader will nevertheless expect you to see and make every possible argument for the other side. Don't permit your personal viewpoint to affect your answer! A good lawyer never does! When discussing an issue, always state the arguments for each side.

Finally, don't forget to ***state your opinion or conclusion*** on each issue. Keep in mind, however, that your opinion or conclusion is probably the ***least*** important part of an exam answer. Why? Because your professor knows that no attorney can tell her client exactly how a judge or jury will decide a particular issue. By definition, an issue is a legal dispute which can go either way. An attorney, therefore, can offer her client only her best opinion about the likelihood of victory or defeat on an issue. Since the decision on any issue lies with the judge or jury, no attorney can ever be absolutely certain of the resolution.

Discuss All Possible Issues

As we've noted, a student should draw ***some*** type of conclusion or opinion for each issue raised. Whatever your conclusion on a particular issue, it is essential to anticipate and discuss ***all of the issues*** which would arise if the question were actually tried in court.

Let's assume that a negligence hypothetical involves issues pertaining to duty, breach of duty, proximate causation, and contributory negligence. If the defendant prevails on any one of these issues, he will avoid liability. Nevertheless, even if you feel strongly that the defendant owed no duty to the plaintiff, you ***must*** go on to discuss all of the other potential issues as well (breach of duty, proximate causation, and contributory negligence). If you were to terminate your answer after a discussion of the duty problem only, you'd receive an inferior grade.

Why should you have to discuss every possible potential issue if you are relatively certain that the outcome of a particular issue would be dispositive of the entire case? Because at the commencement of litigation, neither party can be ***absolutely positive*** about which issues he will win at trial. We can state with confidence that every attorney with some degree of experience has won issues he thought he would lose, and has lost issues on which he thought victory was assured. Since one can never be absolutely certain how a factual issue will be resolved by the factfinder, a good attorney (and exam-writer) will consider *all* possible issues.

To understand the importance of discussing all of the potential issues, you should reflect on what you will do during the actual practice of law. If you represent the defendant, for example, it is your job to raise every possible defense. If there are five potential defenses, and your pleadings only rely on three of them (because you're sure you will win on all three), and the plaintiff is somehow successful on all three issues, your client may well sue you for malpractice. Your client's contention would be that you should be liable because if you had only raised the two additional issues, you might have prevailed on at least one of them, and therefore liability would have been avoided. It is an attorney's duty to raise *all* legitimate issues. A similar philosophy should be followed when taking essay exams.

What exactly do you say when you've resolved the initial issue in favor of the defendant, and discussion of any additional issues would seem to be moot? The answer is simple. You simply begin the discussion of the next potential issue with something like, "Assuming, however, the plaintiff prevailed on the foregoing issue, the next issue would be…" The grader will understand and appreciate what you have done.

The corollary to the importance of raising all potential issues is that you should avoid discussion of obvious non-issues. Raising non-issues is detrimental in three ways: first, you waste a lot of precious time; second, you usually receive absolutely no points for discussing a point which the grader deems extraneous; third, it suggests to the grader that you lack the ability to distinguish the significant from the irrelevant. The best guideline for avoiding the discussion of a non-issue is to ask yourself, "would I, as an attorney, feel comfortable about raising that particular issue or objection in front of a judge?"

Delineate the Transition from One Issue to the Next

It's a good idea to make it easy for the grader to see the issues which you've found. One way to accomplish this is to cover no more than one issue per paragraph. Another way is to underline each issue statement. Provided time permits, both techniques are recommended.

One frequent student error is to write a two-paragraph answer in which all of the arguments for one side are made in the initial paragraph, and all of the rebuttal arguments by the other side are made in the next paragraph. This is *a bad idea*. It obliges the grader to reconstruct the exam answer in his mind several times to determine whether all possible issues have been discussed by both sides. It will also cause you to state the same rule of law more than once. A better-organized answer presents a given argument by one side and follows that immediately in the same paragraph with the other side's rebuttal to that argument.

Understanding the "Call" of a Question

The statements *at the end of* an essay question or of the fact pattern in a multiple-choice question are sometimes referred to as the "call" of the question. It usually asks you to do something specific like "discuss..." "discuss the rights of the parties..." "what are X's rights?..." "advise X..." "the best grounds on which to find the statute unconstitutional are..." "D can be convicted of..." "how should the estate be distributed?...", etc. The call of the question should be read carefully because it tells you exactly what you're expected to do. If a question asks, "what are X's rights against Y?" or "X is liable to Y for..." you don't have to spend a lot time discussing Y's rights against Z. You will usually receive absolutely no credit for discussing facts that are not required by the question. On the other hand, if the call of an essay question is simply "discuss" or "discuss the rights of the parties" then *all* foreseeable issues must be covered by your answer.

Students are often led astray by an essay question's call. For example, if you are asked for "X's rights against Y..." or to "advise X...", you may think you should discuss only X's viewpoint on the issues. This is *not correct*! You cannot resolve one party's rights against another party without considering the issues which might arise (and the arguments which the other side would assert) if litigation occurred. In short, although the call of the question may appear to focus on one of the parties to the litigation, a superior answer will cover all the issues and arguments which that person might *encounter* (not just the arguments she would *make*) in attempting to pursue her rights against the other side.

The Importance of Analyzing the Question Carefully before Writing

The overriding *time pressure* of an essay exam is probably a major reason why many students fail to analyze a question carefully before writing. Five minutes into the allocated time for a particular question, you may notice that the person next to you is writing furiously. This thought then flashes through your mind, "Oh, my goodness, he's putting down more words on the paper than I am, and therefore he's bound to get a better grade." It can be stated *unequivocally* that there is no necessary correlation between the number of words on your exam paper and the grade you'll receive. Students who begin their answer after only five minutes of analysis have probably seen only the most obvious issues, and missed many, if not most, of the subtle ones. They are also likely to be less well organized.

Opinions differ as to how much time you should spend analyzing and outlining a question before you actually write the answer. We believe that you should spend at least 12-18 minutes analyzing, organizing, and outlining a one-hour question before writing your answer. This will usually provide sufficient time to analyze and organize the question thoroughly *and* enough time to write a relatively complete answer. Remember that each word of the question must be scrutinized to determine if it (i) suggests an issue under the operative rules of law, or (ii) can be used in making an argument for the resolution of an issue. Since you can't receive points for an issue you don't spot, it is usually wise to read a question *twice* before starting your outline.

When to Make an Assumption

The instructions on an exam may tell you to *"assume"* facts which are necessary to the answer. Even where these instructions are *not* specifically given, you may be obliged to make certain assumptions with respect to missing facts in order to write a thorough answer. Assumptions should be made when you, as the attorney for one of the parties described in the question, would be obliged to solicit additional information from your client. On the other hand, assumptions should *never be used to change or alter the question*. Don't ever write something like "if the facts in the question were …, instead of …, then … would result." If you do this, you are wasting time on facts which are extraneous to the problem before you. Professors want you to deal with *their* fact patterns, not your own.

Don't assume that your professor has inadverently or accidentally omitted some fact that you think essential to the correct answer. Actually, your professor may have omitted the facts deliberately to see if you *can figure out what to do* under the circumstances. (True, in some instances, your professor may have omitted the facts inadvertently. Even law professors are sometimes human).

The way to deal with the omission of essential information is to describe (i) what fact (or facts) are missing, and (ii) why that information is important. As an example, go back to the "movie shoot" hypothetical we discussed above. In that fact pattern, there was no mention of the relative strength of A and C. This fact could be extremely important. If C weighed 240 pounds and was built like a professional football linebacker, while A tipped the scales at a mere 160 pounds, punching A in the face after he had been pushed to the ground would probably constitute unnecessary force (thereby causing C to forfeit the prevention-of-crime privilege). If the physiques of the parties were reversed, however, C's punch to A's face would probably constitute reasonable behavior. Under the facts, C had to deal the *"knockout"* blow while the opportunity presented itself. The last sentences of the Second Student Answer above show that the student understood these subtleties and correctly stated the essential missing facts and assumptions.

Assumptions should be made in a manner which keeps the other issues open (*i.e.*, necessitates discussion of all other possible issues). Don't assume facts which would virtually dispose of the entire hypothetical in a few sentences. For example, suppose that A called B a "convicted felon" (a statement which is inherently defamatory, *i.e.,* a defamatory statement is one which tends to subject the plaintiff to hatred, contempt or ridicule). If A's statement is true, he has a complete defense to B's action for defamation. If the facts don't tell whether A's statement was true or not, it would *not* be wise to write something like, "We'll assume that A's statement about B is accurate, and therefore B cannot successfully sue A for defamation." So facile an approach would rarely be appreciated by the grader. The proper way to handle this situation would be to state, "if we assume that A's statement about B is not correct, A can not raise the defense of truth." You've communicated to the grader that you recognize the need to assume an essential fact and that you've assumed it in such a way as to enable you to proceed to discuss all other potential issues.

Case Names

A law student is ordinarily *not* expected to recall case names on an exam. The professor knows that you have read several hundred cases for each course, and that you would have to be a memory expert to have all of the names at your fingertips. If you confront a fact pattern which seems similar to a case which you have reviewed (but you cannot recall the name of it), just write something like, "One case held that ..." or "It has been held that ..." In this manner, you have informed the grader that you are relying on a case which contained a fact pattern similar to the question at issue.

The only exception to this rule is in the case of a landmark decision. Landmark opinions are usually those which change or alter established law.[2] These cases are usually easy to identify, because you will probably have spent an entire class period discussing each of them. *Palsgraf v. Long Island Rail Road* is a prime example of a landmark case in Tort law. In these special cases, you may be expected to remember the case by name, as well as the proposition of law it stands for. However, this represents a very limited exception to the general rule which counsels against wasting precious time trying to memorize case names.

---

2. The only subject to which this does not apply is Constitutional Law, since here virtually every case you study satisfies this definition. Students studying Constitutional Law should try to associate case names with holdings and reproduce them in their exam answers.

How to Handle Time Pressures

What do you do when there are five minutes left in the exam and you have only written down two-thirds of your answer? One thing *not* to do is write something like, "No time left!" or "Not enough time!" This gets you nothing but the satisfaction of knowing you have communicated your personal frustrations to the grader. Another thing *not* to do is insert the outline you may have made on scrap paper into the exam booklet. Professors rarely will look at these items.

First of all, it is not necessarily a bad thing to be pressed for time. The person who finishes five minutes early has very possibly missed some important issues. The more proficient you become in knowing what is expected of you on an exam, the greater the difficulty you may experience in staying within the time limits. Second, remember that (at least to some extent) you're graded against your classmates' answers and they're under exactly the same time pressure as you. In short, don't panic if you can't write the "perfect" answer in the allotted time. Nobody does!

The best hedge against misuse of time is to *review as many old exams as possible*. These exercises will give you a familiarity with the process of organizing and writing an exam answer, which, in turn, should result in an enhanced ability to stay within the time boundaries. If you nevertheless find that you have about 15 minutes of writing to do and five minutes to do it in, write a paragraph which summarizes the remaining issues or arguments you would discuss if time permitted. As long as you've indicated that you're aware of the remaining legal issues, you'll probably receive some credit for them. Your analytical and argumentative skills will already be apparent to the grader by virtue of the issues that you have previously discussed.

Write Legibly

Make sure your answer is legible. Students should *not* assume that their professors will be willing to take their papers to the local pharmacist to have them deciphered. Remember, your professor may have 75-150 separate exam answers to grade. If your answer is difficult to read, you will rarely be given the benefit of the doubt. On the other hand, a legible, well-organized paper creates a very positive mental impact upon the grader.

Many schools allow students to type their exams. There are, however, a few disadvantages to typing. For one thing, all the typists are usually in a single room. If the clatter of other typewriters will make it difficult for you to concentrate, typing is probably *not* wise. To offset this problem, some students wear earplugs during the exam. Secondly, typing sometimes makes it difficult to change or add to an earlier portion of your answer. You may have to withdraw your paper from the carriage and insert another. Try typing out a few practice exams before you decide to type your exam. If you do type, be sure to leave at least one blank line between typewritten lines, so that handwritten changes and insertions in your answers can be made easily.

If you decide against typing, your answer will probably be written in a "bluebook" (a booklet of plain, lined, white paper which has a light blue cover and back). It is usually a good idea to write only on the odd numbered pages (*i.e.*, 1, 3, 5, etc.). You may also want to leave a blank line between each written line. Doing these things will usually make the answer easier to read. If you discover that you have left out a word or phrase, you can insert it into the proper place by means of a caret sign ("^"). If you feel that you've omitted an entire issue, you can write it on the facing blank page. A symbol reference can be used to indicate where the additional portion of the answer should be inserted. While it's not ideal to have your answer take on the appearance of a road map, a symbol reference to an adjoining page is much better than trying to squeeze six lines into one, and will help the grader to discover where the same symbol appears in another part of your answer.

The Importance of Reviewing Prior Exams

As we've mentioned, it is ***extremely important to review old exams***. The transition from blackletter law to essay exam can be a difficult experience if the process has not been practiced. Although this book provides a large number of essay and multiple-choice questions, ***don't stop here***! Most law schools have recent tests on file in the library, by course. We strongly suggest that you make a copy of every old exam you can obtain (especially those given by your professors) at the beginning of each semester. The demand for these documents usually increases dramatically as "finals time" draws closer.

The exams for each course should be scrutinized ***throughout the semester.*** They should be reviewed as you complete each chapter in your casebook. Generally, the order of exam questions follows the sequence of the materials in your casebook. Thus, the first question on a law school test may involve the initial three chapters of the casebook; the second question may pertain to the fourth and fifth chapters, etc. In any event, ***don't wait*** until the semester is nearly over to begin reviewing old exams.

Keep in mind that no one is born with the ability to analyze questions and write superior answers to law school exams. Like any skill, it is developed and perfected only through application. If you don't take the time to analyze numerous examinations from prior years, this evolutionary process just won't occur. Don't just ***think about*** the answers to past exam questions; take the time to ***write the answers down***. It's also wise to look back at an answer a day or two after you've written it. You will invariably see (i) ways in which the organization could have been improved, and (ii) arguments you missed.

As you practice spotting issues on past exams, you will see how rules of law become the sources of issues on finals. As we've already noted, if you don't **understand** how rules of law translate into issues, you won't be able to achieve superior grades on your exams. Reviewing exams from prior years should also reveal that certain issues tend to be lumped together in the same question. For instance, where a fact pattern involves a false statement made by one person about another, three potential theories of liability are often present — defamation, invasion of privacy, and intentional infliction of severe emotional distress. You will need to see if any or all of these apply to the facts.

Finally, one of the best means of evaluating if you understand a course (or a particular area within a subject) is to attempt to create a hypothetical exam for that topic. Your exam should contain as many issues as possible. If you can write an issue-packed exam, you probably know that particular area of law. If you can't, then you probably haven't yet acquired an adequate understanding of how the principles of law in that subject can spawn issues.

As Always, a Caveat

The suggestions and advice offered in this book represent the product of many years of experience in the field of legal education. We are confident that the techniques and concepts described in these pages will help you prepare for, and succeed, at your exams. Nevertheless, particular professors sometimes have a preference for exam-writing techniques which are not stressed in this work. Some instructors expect at least a nominal reference to the *prima facie* elements of all pertinent legal theories (even though one or more of those principles is *not* placed into issue). Other professors want their students to emphasize public policy considerations in the arguments they make on a particular issue. Because this book is intended for nationwide consumption, these individualized preferences have *not* been stressed. The best way to find out whether your professor has a penchant for a particular writing approach is to ask her to provide you with a model answer to a previous exam. If an item is not available, speak to upperclass students who received a superior grade in that professor's class.

One more point. While the rules of law stated in the answers to the questions in this book have been drawn from commonly used sources (*i.e.*, casebooks, hornbooks, etc.), it is still conceivable that they may be slightly at odds with those taught by your professor. In instances where a conflict exists between our formulation of a legal principle and the one which is taught by your professor, *follow the latter!* Since your grades are determined by your professors, their views should always supersede the views contained in this book.

Note on Law to Use

The answers to both the essay and the multiple-choice questions in this book assume that the only statute on point is the *Uniform Probate Code* ("UPC"). Where there is no UPC provision on point, you should apply common-law principles.

Where a question involves the rights of spouses, you should assume you're in a common-law property (not community property) jurisdiction. (Alternatively, you can assume that the state follows community property principles, but further assume that all property is the testator's separate property.)

References in the answers to "Haskell" are to Paul Haskell, *Preface to Wills, Trusts & Administration,* 2nd Ed. (Foundation Press 1994).

Essay Exam Questions

Question 1

On July 1, 1983, Tom properly executed a will, which created a $50,000 trust for Lil, the 65-year-old widow of Tom's brother Bob, who died without issue. The Trustee was directed to pay to Lil "as much of the income and, if income be insufficient, as much of the principal, as may be required for her proper support and maintenance, for so long as she lives." After providing for the remainder interest in this trust to go to the American Red Cross on Lil's death, Tom gave "the rest and residue of my estate to the surviving issue of my brothers, per stirpes."

On July 1, 1986, while Tom was confined to the hospital for major surgery, a new will was delivered to Tom in a sealed envelope by two secretaries from his attorney's office. One of them told Tom, "We have a will here that Attorney Smith has asked us to deliver to you for your signature, and which we are to witness." Tom opened the envelope, read the document carefully, and then signed it at the end in front of the secretaries. He then handed it to them. The secretaries walked to a small table in the hallway around the corner from Tom's room, signed the paper on the lines provided for their signature, and then immediately returned the paper to Tom. Under the new will, nephew E was made the sole residuary beneficiary; the rest of the will remained the same as the 1983 will. The 1986 will did not expressly revoke the 1983 will.

Tom died in an automobile accident last month. He was never married and left no issue. He is survived by:

1. A and B, grandchildren of his deceased brother Sam and children of Sam's deceased son James;

2. C, son of his deceased brother John; and

3. D and E, children of his deceased brother Frank.

The original of the 1983 will was found in Tom's safe deposit box. It bears no evidence of acts of revocation. The 1986 will cannot be found but an unsigned copy is in Attorney Smith's possession. The $50,000 trust produces a net annual income of $6,000.

1. Which will, if either, should be admitted to probate? Discuss.

2. Except for the $50,000 trust, what difference, if any, does it make to the family whether they take under the 1983 will or under the laws of intestacy? Discuss.

3. Lil's support needs are approximately $1,000 per month; she has pension and other income of $500 per month and has been making up the difference by withdrawals from savings. If either will is admitted to probate, should the trustee pay Lil $1,000 per month or $500 per month? Discuss.

Question 2

Henry died in the year 2000, leaving an estate consisting entirely of his separate property, valued at $500,000. He is survived by his wife Wanda, his mother Maude, his daughter Sally (by a previous marriage), and his brother Budi. A typewritten will that Henry executed on April 15, 1990, has been filed with the court, and reads as follows:

> "Will of Henry
>
> 1. I give $5,000 to my daughter, Sally.
>
> 2. I give the rest of my estate to my mother, Maude.
>
> 3. I appoint my friend Wanda as executrix of my will."

The will was published and signed by Henry in the presence of Wanda and Sally who, in Henry's presence and in the presence of each other, signed as subscribing witnesses.

Wanda and Henry were married on January 15, 1991. Shortly thereafter, Henry's lawyer, Lana, prepared a new will for Henry, and that will was properly executed in Lana's office on January 30, 1991. That will left Henry's entire estate to Wanda. The original of that will has not been found, but a photocopy is in Lana's files, and it contains a clause expressly revoking all prior wills.

If called as a witness, Lana will testify that (1) the photocopy in her file is a correct copy of the 1991 will, and (2) in December 1999, she tore up the original of the 1991 will at Henry's direction and in his presence.

If called as a witness, Lana's law clerk, Charles, will testify that: he was called into Lana's office one day in December 1999, when Lana and Henry were both present; that Lana told him that the scraps of paper on the desk were Henry's 1991 will, which she had destroyed at Henry's request; and that Henry then nodded his head affirmatively and said, "Now things are back the way I want them; Wanda won't get a penny of my property."

Assuming Lana and Charles testify as above stated and their testimony is properly admitted, how should Henry's estate be distributed? Discuss.

Question 3

The following events all occurred in State Y.

In 1970, Lear, a widower, executed a valid will which read in part: "I leave my AT&T stock to my sister, Ann, and the residue of my estate to my sons, Ed and Frank, equally." The will was executed in duplicate. Lear kept one executed original and his attorney kept the other duplicate original.

When the will was executed, Lear's son Frank was a reformed alcoholic. Through the years, Lear often threatened, in the presence of various family members, to disinherit Frank if he ever returned to drinking again.

In 1987, Lear was walking with his son Ed, when he saw an obviously inebriated person staggering from a bar. Lear, who had poor eyesight, said, "That looks like Frank." Seizing the opportunity to improve his position, believing (but not being positive) that the person was *not* Frank, Ed said, "It sure looks like Frank."

The next day Lear questioned Frank about the incident at the bar. Frank denied being there and accused Lear of being "a paranoid old fogie." Later that same day, Lear asked his new lawyer to prepare a new will and the new will was properly executed. The will read in part: "I revoke all prior wills. I bequeath my AT&T stock to my sister, Ann, and the residue of my estate to my son, Ed. I leave nothing to my son, Frank." Five days later, Lear tore up his copy of the 1970 will and delivered the new will to Ed for safekeeping.

In 1988, Lear suffered extensive brain damage in an automobile accident. Soon thereafter, he was declared mentally incompetent. Ed was appointed guardian for his father, with power to manage and invest his assets. With court approval, Ed sold the AT&T stock and reinvested the proceeds in a comparable security.

Lear has just died. The executed duplicate original of the 1970 will retained by the first attorney and the 1987 will delivered to Ed are both offered for probate.

Assume the applicable statutory law of State Y is the same as comparable provisions of the Uniform Probate Code.

How should Lear's estate be distributed? Discuss.

Question 4

Three years ago, Alfred Dinsmore executed a will which contained the following provisions:

(1) I give my government bonds to Yale College;

(2) I give ten percent of the balance of my estate to my nephew, John, on the condition that he is still married, at the time of my death, to his present wife, Kathleen;

(3) I give the residue of my estate to my niece, Barbara.

Early last year, Alfred wrote the following letter to his niece, Barbara:

I have established a trust for your children at ABC Bank. This trust is worth approximately $50,000 and is composed of all my U.S. and State X bonds. You can decide how these funds should be used.

This is the only document evidencing Alfred's intention to establish a trust. Barbara's two children, Carol and David, are minors.

When Alfred wrote his will, he owned U.S. bonds worth $20,000, State X bonds worth $30,000, and State Z bonds worth $50,000. Alfred died a few weeks ago. At his death, all of these bonds were still registered in his name and had never been out of his possession.

John and Kathleen were divorced three months before Alfred's death, which was unexpected.

At his death, Alfred was unmarried and was survived by his nephew, John, who had no children, his niece Barbara, and Barbara's two children, Carol and David.

1. What are the rights of John and Barbara and of Barbara's children? Discuss.

2. If the court finds a valid trust created by Alfred's letter to Barbara, what are Yale's rights? Discuss.

Question 5

Bill, a widower, purchased a $100,000 farm (Blackacre), bought a single payment life insurance policy on his own life (face amount $50,000), and maintained a large balance in his checking account (usually $100,000). Title to the farm and the bank account were always in Bill's name only. Bill's only child, June, was originally named as beneficiary of the insurance policy, but Bill reserved the power to change the beneficiary.

In 1983, Bill signed a formal change of beneficiary form and sent it to his insurance company. The form changed the beneficiary to Joe, Bill's neighbor. After the company informed Bill that the change had been made, Bill wrote Joe: "I have named you my life insurance beneficiary. You collect the proceeds and divide them three ways. You are one; the others I will name later." Joe replied: "Sure, I'll do what you want."

In 1986, Bill executed a deed conveying Blackacre to an old friend, Pete. Later that same day, Bill mailed a signed letter to Pete, directing him to "rent my farm, pay the net income to June yearly, and when she dies, convey the farm to my church." Pete received and read the letter.

A few days later, Bill attempted to deliver the deed to Pete, but learned from Pete's housekeeper that Pete had just left on a three-month sailing trip in the South Pacific. Bill gave the housekeeper the deed and told her to give it to Pete when he returned.

Last month, Bill suffered a heart attack. While he was hospitalized, he executed a valid will which left "all property I own to my daughter, June. I recommend that she look after my 90-year-old Aunt Selma, as long as she lives, making such gifts and provisions for her as she, June, thinks best."

The day after executing this will, Bill wrote the following on a separate piece of paper: "To Joe: the other two beneficiaries are Tom Allen and his wife." Bill did not sign this note.

Bill died the day after he executed the note to Joe. Two days after Bill's death, Pete returned from his trip and his housekeeper handed Pete the deed.

Who is entitled to Bill's assets and why? Discuss.

Question 6

Ten years ago, Daniel, a widower, executed a valid, typed will containing the following dispositive provisions:

> 1. I give $5,000 to my daughter, Alice.
>
> 2. I give $10,000 to my brother, John.
>
> 3. I give the residue of my estate to my son, Bill. It is my wish that my son use whatever portion of the residue of my estate he deems appropriate to provide for my sister Karen.

John was one of the two witnesses to Daniel's will.

Shortly before the execution of the will, Daniel and John orally agreed that John would convey any property he would receive under Daniel's will to Daniel's sister, Lois.

One year after executing the will, Daniel drew an ink line through the "$5,000" figure in the bequest to Alice, and then wrote above it in ink the figure "$50,000." Daniel also wrote his initials next to the "$50,000" figure.

For many years prior to his death, Daniel had made regular payments to Karen to help her meet ordinary living expenses.

Daniel recently died and is survived by his children, Alice and Bill, and by his brother, John, and sisters, Karen and Lois. His net estate is $100,000.

What are the rights of Alice, Bill, John, Karen and Lois to Daniel's estate? Discuss.

Question 7

Agatha loaned $300,000 to her brother, George. George never repaid any part of the loan. When he died three years later, George left a will which provided that if Agatha forgave the $300,000 debt in writing, a $300,000 trust would be created for her by his executor under his will (Trust #1). Agatha forgave the debt and agreed to look to the trust instrument instead. Under the trust, Agatha is to receive the income for life. Upon her death the corpus is to be distributed to Betty, Agatha's daughter.

After making several other specific bequests, George left his residuary estate in Trust #2, for the benefit of five named beneficiaries. Agatha was not included as a beneficiary of this trust.

Both of the trusts created by George's will contained spendthrift provisions stating that creditors could not reach the income in the trustee's hands.

Nancy, George's accountant, was designated trustee of Trust #1, and Agatha was designated trustee of Trust #2. Each trustee was authorized to sell trust assets.

Before George's death, Agatha borrowed $15,000 from John, a fellow worker. Agatha repaid $5,000 to John and then defaulted. John, who knew about the trust for Agatha, asked her to use her income from the trust to cure the default. She told John that the spendthrift provision prevented her from doing that, but she offered, instead, to sell John 100 shares of TT & A stock from the corpus of Trust #2 for $10,000. The fair market value of the stock was then $21,000. John agreed and purchased the stock from Agatha as trustee of Trust #2 with a check for $10,000.

Six months later, John gave the TT & A stock to his nephew Larry as a wedding present. Larry had no notice of the prior transactions and still has possession of the stock.

What are the rights and liabilities of John, Agatha, and Larry? Discuss.

Question 8

Thirty years ago, Thea executed a trust instrument for "my children," naming State Bank as trustee. At the time of execution, Thea was pregnant with her first child by her husband, Fred.

Thea delivered 80 shares of Disney stock to the Bank under the trust. The trust instrument provided for distribution to Thea's "children" in equal shares upon Thea's death.

Thea died last month. She is survived by her two youngest children. Her oldest child, who was born shortly after the creation of the trust, died two years ago, leaving one son, who also survived Thea.

Eight years ago, Thea executed a valid will in which she gave 100 shares of Disney stock to her husband Fred "out of shares held by me at my death," and "the residue of my estate to my children in equal shares." Six years ago, after she and Fred were divorced, Thea executed a valid codicil. In her codicil, she revoked the gift to Fred and gave 100 shares of Disney stock to her close friend Sal "out of shares held by me at death."

When she executed her will, Thea personally owned 100 shares of Disney stock. After the codicil was executed, a one-for-two stock dividend was declared and issued, and Thea owned 150 shares of Disney stock at her death. After Thea's death, a two-for-three stock dividend was declared, so that her estate held 250 shares at the time of distribution. The trust held 120 shares of Disney stock at Thea's death and, as a result of the two-for-three stock dividend, now holds 200 shares.

Assume that the jurisdiction's applicable statutory provisions are the same as comparable provisions of the Uniform Probate Code.

How should Thea's estate and the trust assets be distributed? Discuss.

Question 9

Alice's husband died more than twenty years ago. Ten years after his death, Alice executed a written instrument transferring $200,000 to Bank in trust for her son Daniel, then 25, and her sister Celia, then 40. Under the terms of the trust, Celia and Daniel were each to receive one-half the income for ten years, at the end of which, each was to receive one-half the principal and any accumulated and undistributed income. If either died during the ten year period, then, at his or her death, his or her share would be distributed to his or her estate.

Six years ago, Phil, a building contractor, sued Celia for $40,000. While the suit was pending, Alice, Bank, Celia and Daniel, executed a written agreement which amended the trust instrument by adding the following:

"No interest hereunder (i) shall be assigned or alienated by any beneficiary, or (ii) shall be subject to the claims of any creditor of any beneficiary." After the amendment was executed, Phil obtained a judgment against Celia for $40,000. Celia was insolvent (apart from her interest in the trust) and could not pay the judgment. Phil has tried to attach Celia's interest in the trust to satisfy the judgment.

A year ago, Alice executed a valid will. The will gave $100,000 to Bank as trustee under Alice's trust, $50,000 in cash to Celia, and the remainder of the estate to her old friend Stan. One of the two attesting witnesses to the will was Doris, Celia's daughter. Celia died 6 months ago. Alice died one month ago.

Alice's only surviving heirs are Doris and Daniel.

In probate proceedings, Daniel asserts the invalidity of Alice's will on the following grounds:

(A) Daniel is not mentioned in the will;

(B) The $100,000 bequest to Bank as trustee should fail because the trust document was not executed in compliance with the Statute of Wills;

(C) The $50,000 bequest to Celia lapsed at her death, and Doris has no claim because she was a witness to the will.

1. How should Alice's estate be distributed? Discuss.

2. Can Phil still reach Celia's interest in the trust? Discuss.

Question 10

Ten years ago, Tina, her husband Hector, and their two adult children, Charlie and Sally, were residents of the State of Terra. They lived in a house owned by Tina. At that time, Tina wrote, dated and signed her will entirely in her own handwriting. The will provides:

> I want my house to go to my daughter, Sally. All my other property of any kind is to go to my husband, Hector, if he survives me, and otherwise to Sally.

Sally acted as witness to Tina's signing and dating of the will and then added her signature under the word "witness." Terra requires that a handwritten will be witnessed and signed by two witnesses.

Charlie died eight years ago. He was survived by his one-year-old son, George. Five years ago, Tina and Hector moved to the State of Calco. A year later, Hector died intestate. Shortly thereafter, Tina gave Sally $300,000 for the purchase of a home. At the time of the gift, Tina stated in writing that the gift was an advancement.

Recently, Tina died while still a resident of Calco. She never revoked or modified her will. Tina was survived by Sally and by George, who was living with his mother in Terra and whom Tina had never seen. When Tina died, her house in Calco was worth $200,000. Her other assets were worth a total of $50,000.

You may assume that the Probate Code of the State of Calco is the same as the Uniform Probate Code.

1. Is Tina's will effective in Calco? Discuss.

2. How should the assets of Tina's estate be distributed? Discuss.

Question 11

Tippi, a very wealthy woman, decided to endow a public library in her home city. To carry out her plan, Tippi executed the following documents:

1. A declaration stating her intention to create the "Tippi Library" for the use of the inhabitants of the city. She designated as "trustees" three persons to serve on the first "Tippi Library Board of Governors" (the "Board"), and provided for the selection of successor members of the Board in the event of death or resignation of a member or members;

2. A deed conveying a block of land Tippi owned near the city center to the Board, "in perpetuity," for the purposes stated in her declaration;

3. A check payable to the Board in the sum of $100,000, as an initial contribution for the library; and

4. A document containing an itemized list of a number of Tippi's stocks and bonds having a market value of $2 million, and a statement that these stocks and bonds were to be delivered to the Board in specified installments over a two-year period.

The declaration, check and deed, and the securities list, have all been delivered to the Board. The Board has recorded the deed, cashed the check, and deposited the proceeds in a bank account entitled "Tippi Library Board." No funds have been withdrawn from, or charged to, the account.

Tippi died three months after all these events occurred, but before any transfers of securities to the Board under the document for specified installments. Tippi left a valid will naming her only child, Betty, as executrix and sole beneficiary. Tippi's husband predeceased her.

The $100,000 fund held by the Board is not sufficient to construct a library building on the land or to maintain a library. If the specified stocks and bonds are transferred to the Board, a library building can be constructed and the library maintained.

The Board has proposed to use the block of land as a public park if it fails in its efforts to get Tippi's stocks and bonds. The park will be named "Tippi Memorial Park." The funds now in the Board's possession are sufficient to maintain the land as a public park for at least ten years.

Betty has brought suit (1) to recover the block of land and all the money in the Tippi Library Board bank account, and (2) for a declaratory judgment that all of the stocks and bonds on Tippi's itemized list are free from any claim by the Board. The Board has responded by asserting all applicable rights and defenses.

To what relief, if any, are Betty and the Board entitled? Discuss.

Question 12

Leonard and Fay Woods had two children, Michael and Linda. Michael was married to Wanda, and they had one adopted child, Roberta. Linda was unmarried and childless. On March 25, 1985, Fay executed a will, with the necessary legal formalities, which contained the following provisions:

> To my daughter, Linda, I give my business property at 1125 Main Street, and such of my jewelry as is enumerated on the list which will be found in my jewel box. To my son, Michael, I give my 1000 shares of XYZ Class A stock. To my husband, Leonard, I give the rest and residue of my estate.

Leonard and Fay were divorced in November 1986. They had not entered into a property settlement agreement. In January 1987, Michael was killed in a plane crash. In April 1987, Fay sold the business property at 1125 Main Street for $20,000 and deposited one-half the proceeds in her commercial account and the other one-half in a savings account in the name of "Fay Woods, Trustee for Linda Woods." In May 1987, XYZ Corporation declared a stock dividend of one-half share of Class A stock and one-half share of Class B stock for each share of Class A stock held by Fay.

Fay died last month. The following typed note was discovered in her jewel box:

> In accordance with the provisions of my will of March 25, 1985, I want my daughter, Linda, to have the following jewelry found herein: Grandmother Barnes' diamond ring, my wedding rings, and my pearl necklace and earrings.

The note was signed and dated March 25, 1985.

All these events took place, and all of Fay's property was located, in the State of Franklin. Fay's estate, after payment of all taxes, expenses, and debts consists of 1500 shares of XYZ Class A stock, 500 shares of XYZ Class B stock, the jewelry described in the March 25, 1985 note, $10,000 in the savings account in the name of "Fay Woods, Trustee for Linda Woods," and $15,000 in her commercial account. All property was Fay's separate property.

Assume that (1) the applicable statutory law of Franklin is the same as comparable provisions of the Uniform Probate Code, and (2) Fay's parents are no longer living.

How should Fay's estate be distributed? Discuss.

Question 13

The following events all occurred in State Y.

On January 5, 1988, Tess executed a valid and attested will naming Martha, her mother, as her sole beneficiary. In July 1990, Tess married Hubert Jones. Shortly after her marriage, Tess signed a document, entirely in her own handwriting, which reads as follows:

> Codicil to my will of 1/5/88. One-half of my property to my husband Hubert; one-fourth of my property to State University; the rest to my mother.
>
> 8/4/90
> Tess Jones

In January 1992, a son, Sonny, was born to Tess and Hubert. Soon thereafter, Tess became upset by the signs of professionalism in college athletics and, especially, the fact that State University constantly had national championship teams in several sports. After watching State trounce A&M in the Apple Bowl, she signed a document which was entirely in her own handwriting and which read as follows:

> I revoke my codicil of 8/4/90. Nothing to athletic factories like State University. I want to benefit a college that has no athletic program. The one-fourth of my property is to go to Harvale College for academic scholarships.
>
> Tess Jones

Tess died in an auto accident two weeks after making the second codicil. She is survived by Martha, Hubert and Sonny. Her estate, after payment of all taxes, debts and expenses of administration, consists of cash and securities having a total value of $300,000.

Harvale is a private, non-profit college. Unbeknownst to Tess, the Regents of State University had voted to discontinue all intercollegiate athletic programs prior to Tess' execution of the second codicil. However, their decision was not announced until after Tess' death.

Assume that the applicable statutory law of State Y is the same as the comparable provisions of the Uniform Probate Code.

How should Tess' estate be distributed? Discuss.

Question 14

Nelly died a widow, leaving a two-page handwritten will containing two dispository clauses. Clause 1 provided for bequests of $10,000 "to each of my children, Ann, Brad and Charlie." Clause 2 provided that all of Nelly's stocks and bonds be given to Brad, "to be used as we have agreed." Nelly's home and personal effects, together worth $60,000, were not disposed of by the will.

Nelly signed her name on the bottom of page 1 of the will. Page 2 contained only the date in her handwriting and Brad's signature under the word "Witness." When the will was offered for probate, several lines were drawn through Ann's name in Clause 1.

Brad is prepared to testify that several months after signing the will, Nelly, in his presence, drew lines through Ann's name, and told him she wanted to disinherit Ann. Brad is also prepared to testify that he had agreed with Nelly to use the income from the stocks and bonds for Charlie during his life, but that the stocks and bonds were to be Brad's after Charlie's death. Charlie died several months before Nelly, leaving no spouse or descendants.

The estate includes, in addition to Nelly's home and personal effects, $10,000 in cash, and stocks and bonds worth $70,000.

1. Is the will valid? Discuss.

2. How should the estate be distributed? Discuss.

Question 15

Carol lived for many years as a widow. She had a son, Sam, and a daughter, Dot. At the outset, she told her children that she didn't need a will because "you'll share in everything anyway." Twenty years ago, Carol was notified by the Department of Defense that Sam had been killed in Vietnam. Soon after the notice, Carol overcame her reluctance to execute a will and executed a valid testamentary document. The document provides:

> In view of the death of my son, Sam, I leave one-third of my estate to my brother, Tom and my sister, Jane, share and share alike; the remaining two-thirds of my estate I give to my daughter, Dot. The shares of my brother and sister in the portion of my estate allocated to them should be adjusted to reflect any advancements I may make to each of them, as recorded in a book of account which will be found with my will.

In 1986, Carol made gifts of $5,000 to Jane and $10,000 to Tom. In her ledger, which was later found with her will, under the caption "Advancements," Carol erroneously transposed the amounts, so that the entries read:

4/9/86 - Jane $10,000

Tom $5,000

In 1998, the Department of State wrote Carol that it had received reports that Sam was apparently still being held as a prisoner of war, and that efforts were being made to verify his status and to secure his release. Dot, who lived with Carol, intercepted the letter and concealed it.

When Carol died recently, she left a net estate of $270,000. After Carol's death but before Carol's estate could be distributed, Sam was released and returned home.

1. Under what theories can Sam participate in the distribution of the estate? Discuss.

2. To what other relief, if any, is Sam entitled? Discuss.

3. How should Carol's estate be distributed? Discuss.

Question 16

The following events all occurred in State A.

In November 1997, T. Tate, a widower, instructed his lawyer to prepare the following document:

> I, T. Tate, a widower, dispose of all my estate as follows: I give my sister, Sally, one-half, and my favorite nephew, Sally's son, Ron, the other one-half. I have intentionally omitted all of my other heirs.

After reading the document, Tate told the attorney he wanted to think about the matter some more and took the document with him without signing it. A week later, on December 2, 1997, Tate attended a dinner party at Sally's house. After dinner and a few drinks, Tate announced that he wanted to execute his will and took the document from his pocket. Slightly intoxicated, Tate signed and correctly dated the document in the presence of all the dinner guests. Tate then had Sally and two of her guests sign as witnesses.

On January 20, 1998, Tate again consulted his lawyer and told him he wanted a new will prepared, revoking all prior bequests, and leaving his entire estate to the Child Care Foundation (CCF), a recognized charitable organization. While Tate was still in the office, the lawyer had his secretary type a memorandum correctly setting forth Tate's requests. Tate signed that memorandum and gave it to the lawyer.

Tate died of a heart attack three weeks after signing the January 20, 1998 memorandum. The document dated December 2, 1997 was found in Tate's desk. Across the document was the following statement, written in Tate's handwriting: "This will is cancelled; I have made a new will. TT"

Tate was survived by his son, Art, his sister, Sally, and Sally's two sons, Don and Zeke, his only relatives. Tate never had a nephew named Ron.

The applicable statutory law of State A is the same as the Uniform Probate Code.

How should Tate's estate be distributed? Discuss.

Question 17

Tawny, a widow, died a few months ago. In searching through her effects, her children found an undated document in her top desk drawer. The document was in Tawny's handwriting, and was signed by her. It stated:

> "My wishes for the distribution of my estate are described on two pieces of paper which are in the bottom drawer of my desk.
>
> (Signed) Tawny"

In Tawny's bottom desk drawer, the children found the following papers:

Document #1

On a form of deed which Tawny had purchased at a local stationery store, all the necessary ingredients of a valid conveyance of Tawny's house, designating her daughter Ann as grantee. The deed was properly executed. Attached to the deed with a paper clip was a note stating:

> "This is for my beloved daughter. I hope that she enjoys it as much as I have.
>
> (Signed) Tawny
> June 1, 1998."

The note was typewritten, except for Tawny's signature and the date.

Document #2

A paper, dated June 1, 1999, stating:

> All my money — brother Bob
>
> ABC stock — sister Shirley
>
> Jewelry — Ann

The note was typewritten, except that the words "brother Bob" had a handwritten line drawn through them. Above them, in Tawny's handwriting, was written: "son Sam".

Document #3

A handwritten, undated piece of paper, stating at the top "Page 2" and continuing:

> I meant to mention in the first page of my will that everything else should be divided equally among Bob, Shirley and Ann.
>
> (Signed) Tawny"

Tawny was survived by her daughter Ann, her son Sam, her brother Bob, and her sister Shirley.

Tawny's estate consists of: her house, valued at $250,000; furniture located in the house worth $10,000; $100,000 in cash; and $50,000 worth of stock in ABC Corp. She owned no jewelry, but did own a $10,000 diamond and ruby-studded jewelry box. Since the earliest of the above dates. ABC stock has split 3 for 1.

How should Tawny's estate be distributed? Discuss.

Question 18

Silver executed a valid will bequeathing his property to Thompson in trust. At his death, Silver's property consisted of a "bar and grill" which he owned and operated, and 100 shares of stock of Red Company, a corporation listed on the New York Stock Exchange. Silver's will authorized Thompson to make investments "in his discretion" and, at the end of two years, to distribute the principal and accrued interest to those persons who would be employed at the bar and grill at Silver's death. The members of this group, and the amount to be distributed to each, were to be decided by Thompson.

During the first year after the death of Silver, Thompson operated the bar and grill at a $10,000 profit. At the end of the year, Red Company merged into Blue Company, a new enterprise engaged in experimental electronics. All shareholders of Red Company were given the option of receiving the fair market value of their stock, which was $75 per share, or receiving one-half share of Blue Company stock in exchange for each share of Red Company stock. Thompson elected to take the 50 shares of Blue Company stock.

At the end of the second year, Thompson sold all the Blue Company stock for $3,000, its then fair market value. He also sold the bar and grill, which had lost $15,000 during the preceding year.

Thompson determined that Able, Baker and Charley were all the eligible employees of the bar and grill, but Thompson died before he could decide what amount to leave to each.

Silver's next of kin now claim the trust property. Assume a lawsuit to settle all rights and liabilities has been initiated by them. Answer and discuss the following:

1. Who is entitled to the trust estate and in what proportions?

2. Has Thompson committed any breaches of trust for which his estate is liable for surcharge and, if so, in what amount?

Question 19

Trisha Tait personally typed this draft of her will:

September 17, 1985

I, Trisha Tait, being of sound mind, hereby publish this as my last will.

First. To my son, Sal I give my 150 shares of Minco stock.

Second. To my daughter, Diane, I give my 500 shares of Oilco stock.

Third. My personal effects located in the wall safe in my living room, I give to my friend Bill.

Fourth. To my husband, Hoby, I give the rest, residue and remainder of my estate.

Tait did not execute this will. The following appears in Tait's handwriting across the bottom of the draft:

June 15, 1986

Being of sound mind, I adopt my draft will, dated September 17, 1985, written above as my last will. TT.

On July 1, 1986, Oilco merged with Zebco. The Oilco shareholders received one share of Zebco stock in exchange for each share of Oilco stock.

Tait died last month.

Tait's son Sal, died in August, 1990. Sal's sole presently-surviving heirs are: his father, Hoby; his wife, Ann; and his adopted daughter, Helen. After payment of all expenses of administration, taxes, and debts, Tait's estate included only the following: 50 shares of Abco stock (worth $5,000) in the living room wall safe; $100,000 in various bank accounts; personal jewelry in the living room wall safe; 300 shares of Minco stock (worth $60,000), and 500 shares of Zebco stock (worth $15,000) in a bank safe deposit box. The personal jewelry was placed into the wall safe on July 1, 1991.

Assume that the applicable statutory law is the same as the comparable provisions of the Uniform Probate Code.

1. Is there a valid will? Discuss.

2. If the will is valid, how should the estate be distributed? Discuss.

3. If the will is not valid, how should the estate be distributed? Discuss.

4. If Hoby predeceased Tait, and Tait had married John one month before her death, how should the estate be distributed? Discuss.

Question 20

The following events all occurred in State Y.

When Timothy Thomas died on July 20, 1998, three documents were found in an envelope in his safe deposit box.

The first read, in its entirety:

> I, Timothy Thomas, make this will, one-half to my sister Bessie and the other one-half to The Boys Club. Sept. 20, 1995.
>
> Witness: William Wordsworth

The second read:

> I'm changing my previous will — Bessie doesn't need all that — all stocks listed in my black book go to Bessie's child — June 30, 1998.
>
> Timothy Thomas

The third was a black notebook containing accurate records of all of Thomas' purchases and sales of securities. All entries were dated prior to June 30, 1998, with the exception of two entries. These showed a sale of 100 shares of ABC stock and the purchase of 100 shares of XYZ stock, both on July 7, 1998.

Each entry in the black notebook was made by Thomas on the actual date of the corresponding transaction.

All writing in the three documents is in Thomas' handwriting, except the words "Witness: William Wordsworth" in the first document. These words are typewritten.

Thomas was never married. His surviving next of kin are his sister Bessie, and Bessie's daughter, Dorothy.

Thomas' estate consists of the following: 300 shares of ABC stock purchased prior to June 30, 1998, having a fair market value of $30,000; 100 shares of XYZ stock purchased on July 7, 1998, having a fair market value of $10,000; and $100,000 cash in bank accounts.

Assume that the applicable statutory law of State Y is the same as comparable provisions of the Uniform Probate Code.

As among Bessie, The Boys Club, and Dorothy, how should Timothy Thomas' estate be distributed? Discuss.

Question 21

Ten years ago, Tammy Thor, a widow, validly executed a formal, witnessed will (Will #1) which contained the following dispositive clauses:

> (1) to my friend Robert Rood, $10,000 to be used by him for the education of his daughter, Carrie;

> (2) the residue of my estate to my friend Doris Drake, trustee, in trust, to pay the income to my daughter, Ethel, so long as Ethel may live and upon Ethel's death to distribute the trust corpus to my heirs; the trustee may invade the corpus if necessary for the proper care and maintenance of Ethel.

Three years ago, Thor signed a dated, typewritten document purporting to be her last will and testament (Will #2). The document was identical to Will #1, except that the last clause of the residuary bequest, giving the trustee power to invade the corpus, was omitted. This will was attested by only one subscribing witness.

Thor recently died. Will #1 and Will #2 were found in Thor's safe deposit box. Stapled to Will #1 was the following document, in Thor's handwriting:

> This will is hereby cancelled and revoked. I have made a new will.
>
> Tammy Thor

The note was dated, in Thor's handwriting, one day subsequent to the date on Will #2.

Thor was survived by the following heirs and legatees and no others:

(a) her daughter, Ethel;

(b) her friend Robert Rood and Robert's 16-year-old daughter Carrie;

(c) John and Gil, sons of her deceased sister Anne;

(d) Warren, grandson of her deceased sister Bessie;

(e) Doris Drake.

Ethel died before distribution of Thor's estate. By a valid will, Ethel left her entire estate to her friend Sandra.

1. Did Thor die testate or intestate? Discuss.

2. Assuming Thor died testate, what persons are entitled to Thor's estate, and what share or interest will each receive? Discuss.

3. Assuming Thor died intestate, what persons are entitled to Thor's estate, and what share or interest will each receive? Discuss.

Question 22

Ten years ago, Tom, who had never been married, executed a typed will ("Will #1") which gave "$50,000 to my niece, Mary, $15,000 to my nephew, John, $15,000 to my nephew, Allen, and the residue of my estate to my niece and nephews, share and share alike." The will was witnessed by Tom's secretary and his niece, Mary.

Tom had only one niece, Mary, and three nephews, John, Allen and David. David had died before the execution of the will, leaving two surviving children.

After Will #1 was executed, John told Tom on numerous occasions that Allen had been unsuccessful in starting a business, and had become involved in the sale of stolen automobile parts. In fact, John knew that Allen, who had moved to another city and had not been in contact with Tom for some time, owned a successful business and was not engaged in the sale of stolen goods.

After Tom's recent death, a validly executed second will ("Will #2") bearing a date which preceded Tom's death by approximately three years, was found in Tom's safe deposit box. Will #2 gave "$50,000 to my niece Mary, $30,000 to my nephew John, and the residue of my estate to Mary and John, share and share alike."

Will #1, which had lines drawn through each of its provisions, was also found in Tom's safe deposit box.

Tom's only surviving relatives were Mary, John, Allen, and David's two children. Tom's net estate was $200,000.

What are the rights to Tom's estate of Mary, John, Allen, and David's two children. Discuss.

Question 23

Betty and Wilma had been business partners and close friends for many years. Both were widows and each had two children.

In 1990, Betty executed a will in which she bequeathed "$100,000 to my close friend, Wilma, if she survives me; otherwise, to the natural persons who are beneficiaries of Wilma's last will and testament, and if she dies intestate, to her next of kin." The residue of Betty's estate was bequeathed "to my children, share and share alike." In 1994, both of Betty's children died, survived by issue. Her son, Charles, left two sons, George and Fred. Her daughter, Jane, left a daughter, Alice.

Wilma had drawn a will in 1985 leaving her entire estate "one-half to my children and one-half to State University." In 1992, thinking that Bill had failed to thank her for an expensive present (a new Volvo which she had given to Bill), Wilma drew a codicil, providing "I hereby delete from my will the gift to my son, Bill. Because of his ingratitude, I leave him nothing." In fact, Bill had sent Wilma a "thank you" letter, but it had been lost in the mail.

Last week, Betty and Wilma were killed in an airplane crash while en route to a convention. Betty's next of kin were her three grandchildren. Wilma's next of kin were her two children, Bill and Mary.

Betty and Wilma each left a net estate of $500,000 in cash and marketable securities.

Assume the applicable statutory law is the same as comparable provisions of the Uniform Probate Code.

How should their estates be distributed? Discuss.

Question 24

Ball transferred $100,000 in trust to Trust Company for the benefit of his son, Sam. The income was to be distributed to Sam during Sam's life, and the remainder of the trust was to pass to Sam's children living at the time of Sam's death. Ball could, according to the terms of the trust, revoke the trust, provided that the revocation was in writing signed by him and delivered to the trustee. The trust also contained a spendthrift clause.

 After the creation of the trust, Sam married Pearl and they had one child, Carol. Two years after the birth of Carol, Pearl divorced Sam. Pearl took this action because Sam had become a chronic alcoholic. When Ball learned of the divorce and that a large alimony award had been given to Pearl, Ball called the trustee and stated, "I revoke the trust and will confirm this revocation by letter." However, Ball died the following day, before he had written the letter. Ball died intestate. Sam was Ball's only child. Sam has no income apart from that paid to him by the trust.

Trust Company has filed a petition for instructions in the appropriate court. The petition alleges the following:

> (A) That Sam has made written demand that the trustee (1) turn over the entire trust estate, free of trust, to the administrator of Ball's estate, or, in the alternative, (2) out of the income and, to the extent necessary, the principal of the trust, pay Pearl the amount now due her for alimony, and thereafter pay her periodically the amount awarded for future alimony.

> (B) That Pearl has made written demand that the trustee, out of the income and, to the extent necessary, the principal of the trust, pay her the amount now due to her for alimony and thereafter pay her periodically the amount awarded to her for future alimony. In her demand, Pearl states that she represents Carol, now age 3, and, on Carol's behalf, agrees to an invasion of the trust principal for such purpose.

> (C) That Sam and Pearl, jointly, have made a written election, on their own behalf and on behalf of Carol, to terminate the trust, if the trustee does not agree to the foregoing demands.

The trustee requests instructions with respect to the following:

1. Whether the trust was effectively terminated by Ball in his lifetime;

2. Whether the trustee is obligated to pay Pearl either past or future alimony, or both, out of the income and, to the extent necessary, the principal of the trust;

3. Whether Sam and Pearl have the legal power to terminate the trust.

How should the court instruct the trustee? Discuss.

Question 25

The following events all occurred in State Y.

Theresa Taylor died recently. After her death a typewritten document was found in her safe deposit box. It read (in its entirety) as follows:

> To Aunt Marie — my home; to my friend Al — my 200 shares of XYZ stock; to my friend Frank — 20 shares of IBM stock; to my daughter Doris — NOTHING!

Stapled to the typewritten document was another piece of paper on which was written, in Taylor's handwriting: "The attached is the way I want my property to go; all the rest to sister, Sarah. 5-15-90. Theresa Taylor."

Taylor was survived by her daughter Doris, Aunt Marie, Al, Frank and a brother, Ben. Her sister Sarah died in October 1991, without issue, but with a will which left everything to Sarah's husband, Greg.

Taylor's estate consists of: $50,000 cash on deposit in banks (the proceeds of fire insurance relating to her home, which was destroyed by fire two months ago); 400 shares of XYZ stock (200 shares of which were the result of a stock split in August 1988); and government bonds having a fair market value of $100,000. Taylor did not have, and never had owned, any IBM stock.

Assume that the applicable statutory law of State Y is the same as comparable provisions of the Uniform Probate Code.

How should Taylor's estate be distributed after payment of debts, taxes, and expenses of administration? Discuss.

Essay Exam Answers

Answer to Question 1

1. Which will, if either, should be admitted to probate?

Was the 1986 will valid?

The requirements for will execution vary from state to state. The modern trend, reflected in the Uniform Probate Code, is to liberalize the requirements. Under the UPC, a will is valid if it is witnessed by at least two persons, each of whom signed within a reasonable time after he or she witnessed either the testator's signing of the will or the testator's acknowledgment of: (1) his signature or (2) the will itself. (UPC § 2-502). Since (1) Tom ("T") executed the will in front of two legal secretaries who knew the document to be his will, and (2) the secretaries signed the document almost immediately thereafter, the 1986 will was valid when executed. There is (at least, under the UPC and in many jurisdictions) no requirement that the witnesses sign in the presence of the testator (or in the presence of each other), so the fact that the witnesses here signed in the hallway outside of T's hospital room does not affect the validity of the will. In some states, the requirements for validity would be more stringent.

Is the 1986 will deemed revoked by being lost?

If a will which was last seen in the testator's possession (or control) cannot be found upon his death, there is ordinarily a presumption that the testator destroyed the will with the intent to revoke it. The presumption is rebuttable. The presumption does not arise if the will was last known to be in the possession of a third person. The UPC is silent on the issue of lost wills.

T's nephew E can attempt to rebut this presumption by arguing that T knew how to enlist the assistance of Attorney Smith in connection with his will and would have gone back to Smith if he had actually meant to revoke the 1986 will. However, this argument alone would probably *not* be sufficient to rebut the presumption that T had intended to revoke the 1986 will. The fact that T retained the 1983 will in his safe deposit box supports the presumption that he meant to revoke the 1986 will. If he had meant to substitute the 1986 will for the 1983 will, he would have removed the 1983 will from the deposit box and replaced it with the 1986 will.

On these facts alone, we may conclude that the copy of the 1986 will would probably *not* be admitted to probate.

If, however, the 1986 will was not deemed revoked, the court might accept proof of its contents by admitting the unsigned copy in Attorney Smith's possession. Attorney Smith could testify that he gave the original to the two secretaries who visited T; and the secretaries could verify that T had signed the will in their presence.

If the 1986 will is deemed valid, does it revoke the 1983 will?

A subsequent testamentary instrument need not contain a revocation clause to cause the revocation of a prior will. A prior will may be revoked either expressly or because its provisions are inconsistent with the later will. (UPC § 2-507(a)(1)). Even without a revocation clause, a subsequent will wholly revokes a previous will by inconsistency if the testator intended the subsequent will to replace the old one rather than supplement it. (UPC § 2-507(b)). When the later will disposes of the entire estate, that will is presumed to be entirely inconsistent with the earlier will, even if some provisions remain essentially the same in the two wills. (UPC § 2-507(c)). Since the 1986 will purports to dispose of T's entire estate, it will supersede the 1983 instrument if it is deemed valid, and it will be admitted to probate.

If the 1986 will is deemed revoked, is the 1983 will revived?

What happens to an earlier will when a subsequent will which was intended to revoke the earlier will is itself revoked by destruction or loss? In most states the answer is provided by a specific statute. Some states provide that, once revoked, a prior will may not be revived. In other states, the first will is revived when the second will is destroyed, if that was the testator's intent. The UPC adopts the latter view. It states, "...The previous will is revived if it is evident from the circumstances of the revocation of the subsequent will or from the testator's contemporary or subsequent declarations that the testator intended the previous will to take effect as executed." (UPC § 2-509(a)).

Here, there is no evidence that T intended or desired the 1983 will to be reinstated. Although the will was preserved in his safe deposit box, it's possible that T simply neglected to dispose of the 1983 will after the 1986 document was created. However, the aggrieved beneficiaries (*i.e.*, those residuary beneficiaries in the 1983 will who were left out of the 1986 will) might prevail, *if* they could show that T was such a careful and prudent person that he would recognize that his intent would be best expressed by preserving one will and destroying or disposing of the other. On this proof, T's retention of the 1983 will would arguably manifest his desire to have that document constitute his testamentary scheme.

The doctrine of dependent relative revocation is not applicable to these facts. The doctrine comes into play when the Testator revokes an earlier will on the assumption that a subsequent will is valid. If in fact the second will is invalid because of some mistake in the execution or some other mistake, it's assumed that the testator would want the first will restored. Obviously, this is not always the case and the doctrine is difficult for the courts to apply. The doctrine is not applicable here because there is no showing that the 1986 will was executed improperly or that any of its provisions mistakenly stated T's intent at the time of execution.

Summary:

If the 1983 will is restored after the 1986 will is deemed revoked, the surviving issue of T's brothers will take the residue per stirpes. If the 1986 will is admitted after proving the copy, E will take the entire residue. If neither will is admitted, T will be deemed to have died intestate.

2. What is the difference between the disposition in the 1983 will and intestacy?

Under the 1983 will, the surviving issue of T's brothers take as directed by T, i.e, per stirpes (*i.e.*, through the roots of each brother). Conceptually, the residue is divided into three shares, one for each brother who has issue, and then into subshares for the issue of each brother. Thus, A and B would each receive 1/6 of T's residuary estate (*i.e.*, they get equal shares of the 1/3 that James would have gotten as the sole issue of Sam); C would receive a full 1/3 of T's residuary estate (as sole issue of John); and D and E would each get 1/6 (sharing equally the 1/3 that would have gone to Frank). As the facts tell us, brother Bob died without issue.

Any part of a decedent's estate not effectively disposed of by will passes by intestate succession to the decedent's heirs as prescribed by statute in each state. Under the Uniform Probate Code, T's residue would pass to his "descendants by representation," i.e. *per capita* at each generation. (UPC § 2-103(1)). The division of the estate would be made at (and be in equal portions at) the highest level in which there are living members. (UPC § 2-106(b)). Thus, one equal share each would go to C, D, E and one to the issue of deceased James. The final result would be: C, D and E would each get 1/4 of the residuary estate; and A and B would each get 1/8 (splitting James' 1/4 share equally).

[*Note:* For exam questions such as this one (where there are many potential beneficiaries and you are asked to discuss the difference between testamentary and intestate distribution to those beneficiaries), you should diagram the family tree (on scrap paper, not in your exam bluebook) before attempting to answer.] The family tree for this question would look like this:

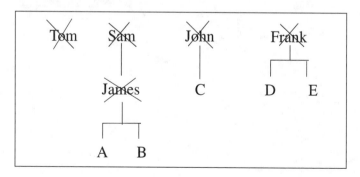

3. *Should Lil receive $1,000 per month, or $500 per month?*

When there are ambiguous provisions in a will or the provisions are capable of different or inconsistent interpretations, the court will attempt to effectuate the testator's intent by inquiring into all the circumstances. Lil could argue that she was intended to be the sole living beneficiary of the trust and that T would naturally prefer her interests to those of a large and well-funded charity. By using the terms "as much of the income, and if income be insufficient, as much of the principal...," T manifested a clear directive to support her from the trust, not to cause her to deplete her savings.

On the other hand, T presumably knew that Lil was receiving funds from other sources. He could have requested Attorney Smith to insert the language, "regardless of Lil's other income" if he had wanted to give a free hand to the trustee. Because (1) the principal would be exhausted in a relatively short period of time if Lil received $12,000 per year from the trust, and (2) the trust was apparently to last for her entire life (the trust language states, "for so long as she lives"), it can be argued that T intended to limit Lil to $500 per month from the trust.

Without additional facts, either interpretation of the will's provision would be reasonable.

Answer to Question 2

We must first decide whether the 1990 will was validly executed, and, if so, whether it was effectively revoked by the 1991 will and, if it was revoked, whether it was revived by the destruction of the 1991 will.

Was the 1990 will executed with the requisite formalities?

The Uniform Probate Code requires that an attested will be in writing, signed by the testator or in the testator's name by some other person in the testator's conscious presence and by the testator's direction, and that it be signed by two persons within a reasonable time after execution. (UPC § 2-502).

Historically, persons interested as legatees or beneficiaries under a will could not serve as witnesses. Today, the rule in most states is still either to (1) automatically disqualify interested witnesses, *or* (2) permit them to qualify, but purge them of their gifts. The UPC and a number of states remove this disqualification (UPC § 2-505(b)). Under the UPC, the 1990 will appears to be valid even though Sally was both a beneficiary and a witness. Wanda's appointment as executor would not affect her qualification as witness, even in a state that does disqualify interested witnesses. The theory is that the executor has a separate interest as recipient of fees for service as fiduciary. (Note: a lawyer who prepares the will and/or is present at the execution is a valid witness.)

Can the 1991 will be proved as a testamentary instrument though the original is not produced?

In most jurisdictions, a will which cannot be produced in court can nevertheless be proved. However, the burden is on the proponents of the will to prove its valid execution and its contents.

In this case, Lana's testimony proves the revocation of the 1991 will, and the reason why it cannot be produced in court. Lana's testimony that the photocopy is a true and correct copy of the 1991 will may be used to establish its terms. Her testimony is supported by the testimony of Lana's law clerk, who saw the torn scraps of the will and heard Henry confirm that he considered the 1991 will ineffective.

Was the 1991 will revoked?

The UPC allows revocation by "revocatory act." The definition of a revocatory act includes "burning, tearing, canceling, obliterating, or destroying the will or any part of it." The burning, tearing or cancellation of a will are revocatory acts even if the acts do not touch any of the words on the will. The acts must be performed by the testator or another person at (i) the testator's direction, and (ii) in his "conscious presence," with the intent of revoking it. UPC § 2-507(a)(2). Lana's testimony, corroborated by Charles, establishes that the will was destroyed by Lana in Henry's presence and at Henry's direction.

Did the revocation of the 1991 will have the effect of reviving the 1990 will?

In many states, revocation of a later testamentary instrument which by its terms revokes a prior testamentary instrument does *not* revive the earlier instrument. The UPC confirms that the previous will "remains revoked, unless it is revived." However, the Code goes on to provide that if the second will was revoked by physical act, the first will is revived if it appears from either: (1) the circumstances of the revocation of the second will, or (2) the testator's contemporaneous or subsequent declarations, that the decedent intended the first will to take effect as executed. UPC § 2-509(a).

Henry's statement, that "things are back the way I want them; Wanda won't get a penny of my property," suggests that his intent was to have the 1990 will revived. Wanda will argue, however, that the statement is too ambiguous to prove an intent to revive the 1990 will. Nevertheless, Henry's statement to Lana and Charles would probably be interpreted to mean that he desired reinstatement of the earlier will rather than intestacy.

How should the estate be distributed?

Assuming the validity and revival of the first will, Wanda will claim that she is entitled to take her elective spousal share as in intestacy.

The rights of a spouse in intestacy are determined in almost all states by elective share statutes. The UPC provides that, if a testator fails to provide for a surviving spouse who married the testator *after* the execution of the will, the omitted spouse receives a full intestate share, unless: (1) it appears *from the will* or other evidence that the will was made in contemplation of the marriage; or (2) the will expresses the intention that it is to be effective notwithstanding any subsequent marriage; or (3) the testator provided for the spouse outside the will with intent that the transfer serve as a substitute for a gift under the will. UPC § 2-301. Since none of these conditions applies here, Wanda will take an intestate share of the estate. Under UPC § 2-102(4), where one or more of the decedent's surviving descendants are not descendants of the surviving spouse (in this case, his daughter Sally), the surviving spouse's intestate share is $100,000 plus one-half of the balance of the estate ($400,000). On these facts, Wanda's total share would be $300,000. The remaining $200,000 would be divided: (1) the specific bequest of $5,000 to Sally, and (2) the residue, $195,000, to Maude. Henry's brother would not share.

In intestacy:

If it is determined that the first will was not revived, the estate would be distributed by intestate succession. This would result in Wanda's receiving $300,000 (as calculated above). The balance of the estate would be distributed to Sally, as Henry's only surviving descendant. Maude and Budi would not share. [Note: Interestingly, the result for Wanda is the same whether or not the 1990 will is valid. Wanda's position is improved only if the 1991 will is effective.]

Answer to Question 3

Was the execution of the 1987 will induced by Ed's fraud? If so, what are Frank's remedies?

The burden of proof on the issue of fraud in the inducement is on the contestant. Frank will have to prove that Lear was induced to make the 1987 will by Ed's fraudulent representation that Frank was the person Lear saw outside the bar.

The Uniform Probate Code has no provision which deals specifically with fraud in the inducement. Under the common law, fraud which induces the execution of a will is defined as reliance by the testator upon a false, material statement of fact made with the intention of deceiving him into inserting provisions in the will which he would not insert in the absence of the deception. In fraud in the inducement, the testator knows the contents of the will. But the contents would be different if he were not deceived. Fraud in the inducement is distinguished from fraud in the execution. An example of fraud in the execution: T tells his lawyer to leave the residue of his estate to A and B. The attorney intentionally substitutes C for B. T executes the will believing it names A and B as his residual beneficiaries.

Frank would argue that the facts show all the elements of fraud in the inducement: (1) Ed lied when he stated that the drunkard looked like Frank when he really believed that the person he saw was *not* Frank; (2) Ed knew that Lear's discovery of Frank's return to alcoholism might lead to his disinheritance by Lear; and (3) Lear relied on Ed's misrepresentation when he changed his will the very next day.

Ed would argue in rebuttal that: (1) Ed could not know the contents of the 1970 will and had no discernible reason to induce Lear to revoke it; and (2) it's possible to conclude that Lear did *not* rely upon Ed's statement in making the new will: (a) Lear asked Frank himself about the incident and Frank had the opportunity to dispel Lear's doubts, and (b) Lear was probably provoked to change his will not by anything Ed said but by Frank's statement that Lear was a "paranoid old fogie."

After reviewing all the facts, the court could reasonably conclude that the execution of the 1987 will was induced by Ed's fraud. The court is likely to rely on Frank's arguments and on the following facts: (1) even if Ed was not aware of the exact disposition of property under Lear's will, he knew how strongly Lear felt about Frank's possible return to drink and had reason to anticipate that Lear would take some action to favor Ed; and (2) the confrontation between Lear and Frank which resulted in Frank's angry response to Lear would not have occurred if Ed had responded to Lear's earlier inquiry truthfully.

In some states, when a new will is determined to be invalid for fraud in the inducement, provisions in the will revoking a prior will fail as well. In those jurisdictions, the 1987 will and its revocatory clause would be void and the 1970 will reinstated (assuming its terms can be proved).

In other states, the remedy for Ed's fraud will be to impose a constructive trust upon one-half of Ed's bequest (*i.e.*, the amount Frank would have received under the 1970 will) for the benefit of Frank.

Will the 1970 will be revived?

If the revocation of the 1970 will in the 1987 will is set aside as having been procured by fraud, the terms of the 1970 will must still be proved. Because the will was executed in duplicate originals, Frank may prove the terms of the 1970 will and its due execution by submission of the duplicate original and the testimony of his attorney. See UPC § 3-402(a).

Did the sale of the AT&T stock by Ed result in ademption of the gift to Ann?

At common law, if a testator left a specific bequest and the subject of the bequest was no longer available at his death, the bequest was said to fail or be "adeemed." The process was called "ademption." Whichever will is admitted here, the other beneficiaries will argue that Ann takes nothing, because the gift to her was adeemed. Ann will attack this contention on two separate grounds.

First, she will argue that the sale of the AT&T stock was intrinsically fraudulent in nature (*i.e.*, Ed deliberately sold the stock to extinguish the gift to Ann). In light of (1) Ed's earlier lies to Lear about Frank, and (2) the fact that he purchased a comparable security with no real purpose to change the nature of Lear's holdings, her arguments will probably prevail. If so, the court would impose a constructive trust in favor of Ann upon Ed's share, in an amount equal to the value of the AT&T stock when distribution would be due to Ann.

Under amendments adopted in 1990, the UPC provides that "if specifically devised property is sold by a conservator, . . . the specific devisee has the right to a general pecuniary devise equal to the net sale price. . . ." (UPC § 2-606(b)). Thus, Ann would have a right to receive the value of the stock out of the general assets of Lear's estate, *if* she can show that the devise to her was specific (rather than general) in nature.

Whether a testamentary gift is specific or general depends upon the testator's intent, as determined from all of the applicable circumstances. Where a testator utilizes the word "my" before a gift of stock, as happened here, some courts will conclude that a specific gift was intended. Others require that the number of shares be specified (which Lear did not do), or even that the words "All of my ...." precede the description of the gift (which Lear also didn't do). Considering all the facts, the court will probably find that the bequest here was specific, and Ann will be entitled to the value of the proceeds from the sale by Ed of the AT&T stock.

Lear's estate would probably be distributed as follows: (a) an amount equal to the sale proceeds of the AT&T stock will be distributed to Ann; and (b) the residue of the estate will be distributed equally between Ed and Frank.

Answer to Question 4

1. What are the rights of John and Barbara and of Barbara's children?

As to John: was the gift to John revoked by failure of the condition?

Barbara will contend that the gift to John was subject to an express condition subsequent which became effective to revoke John's bequest. The condition was that John remain married to Kathleen at Alfred's death.

Unless a condition in a will is deemed against public policy, it will ordinarily be given effect as written. Some conditions are so offensive that they are almost never enforced. Among these are: (1) conditions which restrain a person from marrying, or (2) conditions which encourage divorce. The condition in this case accomplished the very opposite: it encouraged John to preserve his marriage to Kathleen. Because Alfred was childless, he was probably especially concerned to encourage stability in his nephew's life. Also, he may have become fond of Kathleen and wished not to harm her. On these facts, it is likely that the court will enforce the condition as written.

The Uniform Probate Code makes specific provision for devises (other than residuary devises) which fail. The Code provides that a gift which fails for any reason becomes part of the residue of the estate (UPC § 2-604(a)). Since the will provides that Barbara take the residue, John's ten percent interest in the balance of the estate goes to Barbara.

Did Alfred create a valid trust in favor of Barbara's children?

Neither the trust nor Barbara's children are mentioned in the will and more than two years elapsed between execution of the will and the letter to Barbara. Barbara's children will assert that Alfred had continued to review his affairs and that he intended his letter to Barbara to constitute a valid, *inter vivos*, discretionary trust for their benefit. If a valid living trust existed, then the U.S. and State X bonds would not be part of Alfred's estate when he died, and they would not pass to Yale College.

An *inter vivos* trust requires: (1) manifestation of intent by the trustor to create a trust, (2) an identifiable trust res, (3) designation of a trustee, and (4) identifiable trust beneficiaries. The children will argue that all these requirements were satisfied by the letter. Alfred's intent to create a trust is clear and emphatic ("I have established a trust..."). The contents of the trust res are clear. The beneficiaries are unequivocal. A reasonable interpretation of the letter is that Alfred intended himself to be the trustee, but that he would look to Barbara for advice and guidance on the distribution of funds to the children. In the alternative, he intended Barbara to be the trustee and gave her full discretion to distribute the income and corpus of the trust as she wished.

Yale will argue that: (1) Alfred may have thought about creating a trust but changed his mind and finally decided not to; (2) his intent was not to be the trustee himself but to make the bank the trustee, and that his failure to execute the necessary documents at the bank clearly proves his change of heart; (3) that no delivery of the trust res ever occurred (*i.e.*, the U.S. and State X bonds were never delivered to anyone but were retained by Alfred, a clear indication that he meant them to go to Yale as originally planned; and (4) that there is no reasonable basis for concluding that he meant Barbara to be the trustee--the language "I have established a trust..." instead of the equally simple language "I am establishing a trust," shows that he did not intend Barbara to be the trustee.

Barbara's children will argue in rebuttal that Alfred's unequivocal language in his letter to Barbara ("I *have* established a trust for your children . . .composed of all my U.S. and State X bonds.") should control regardless of the trustee's identity. The retention of the bonds by Alfred simply establishes that he was holding them as both his will and the letter would indicate -- the U.S. and State X bonds for the benefit of the children and only the State Z bonds for Yale.

In response, the children will reassert their argument that Alfred intended himself to be the trustee. His statement to Barbara, "You can decide how the funds should be used" meant only that Alfred would consult with Barbara before expending any funds in the children's behalf. Because the trust res (the U.S. bonds and the X bonds only) was clearly identified in Alfred's letter to Barbara, Alfred was not obliged to segregate the bonds from his other assets.

Because the letter to Barbara so clearly designated the components of the trust and so clearly designated the intent to benefit Barbara's children, it's likely that the children will prevail.

If a trust was created with Alfred as trustee, his subsequent death would not cause the trust to fail. A successor trustee (probably Barbara) would simply be appointed.

If, as seems unlikely, no trust at all was created, then the U.S. and State X bonds remained in Alfred's estate at his death and would go to Yale College along with the State Z bonds.

2. *Assuming the creation of a valid trust for Barbara's children, what are the rights of Yale College?*

If a valid trust *was* created by Alfred, the court will have to decide what effect that will have on the testamentary gift to Yale. Specifically, does Yale get cash equal to the value of the U.S. and State X bonds at Alfred's death? To the extent Yale gets cash, the residuary gift to Alfred's niece Barbara will be reduced accordingly.

Under the common law, a specific devise is adeemed — rendered ineffective — if the property which is devised is not owned by the testator at death. Under the common law, Yale would not get cash in lieu of the value of the U.S. and State X bonds. Instead, it would get only the State Z bonds.

The more modern approach, reflected in the UPC, is to apply ademption only where the facts indicate that the testator intended to extinguish the gift or when ademption is "consistent with the testator's manifested plan of distribution." UPC § 2-606(a)(6). Even under this modern/UPC "intent of the testator" approach, however, ademption would probably still apply here. The facts indicate that the bonds were a material part of Alfred's assets; it's unlikely he wanted to drain his estate of a matching amount of cash to Yale, especially since that would come at the sole expense of his niece, Barbara. After the failure of the conditional bequest to his nephew John, Barbara was his principal living heir and we may reasonably presume that he would prefer her.

Yale would, however, be entitled to the State Z bonds, because these are included in the term "government bonds" and were excluded from the contents of the trust.

Answer to Question 5

The proceeds of the insurance policy:

The issue here is whether Joe gets all the proceeds of the policy or whether Tom Allen and his wife each gets one-third of the proceeds. A subsidiary issue is whether the three share as principal beneficiaries or as beneficiaries of a trust of which Joe is the trustee. One thing is clear--June does not get any part of the insurance proceeds. Although she was originally a beneficiary, the change in beneficiaries was effective to remove her. Nor can she claim any part of the proceeds under the will or in intestacy. The proceeds of an insurance policy are *not* part of the insured's estate.

Bill's letter to Joe following his designation as beneficiary expressed Bill's intent to limit Joe's interest in the policy to one-third of the proceeds. His subsequent note to Joe, although unsigned, confirmed this intent by naming the individuals who would share equally in the other two-thirds. It would be difficult under these facts to argue that Joe should get anything more than Bill intended--*i.e.*, one-third and no more than one-third.

Joe will argue that the first letter was ineffective because no specific persons were named to share in the proceeds and that the change of beneficiary form filed with the company controlled the disposition of funds. He will also argue that Bill knew how to accomplish a formal change in beneficiaries and would have done so if he had meant to. He will rely on the fact that the second letter was unsigned and therefore not binding on anyone. Joe is likely to be helped in his arguments by the insurance company, which is unlikely to want to pay the proceeds except as confirmed in the formal designation of beneficiaries. The company will probably deposit the proceeds into court pending the outcome of the litigation.

Tom Allen and his wife will argue that the first letter to Joe, which Joe agreed to respect, constituted a change in beneficiaries which was confirmed and made explicit by the second letter. On this theory, they will claim outright ownership of two-thirds of the insurance proceeds. They will also argue in support of their claim to share in the proceeds outright that they are the third-party beneficiaries of a written agreement between Bill and Joe as expressed in the exchange of letters.

If the claim to receive their share of the proceeds as principal beneficiaries fails, Tom and his wife can then argue that they are the beneficiaries of a trust which arose by reason of Bill's initial letter to Joe, Joe's agreement to be bound by the terms of the letter, and Bill's second letter naming them as beneficiaries. They will argue that Joe became a trustee for the benefit of three designated beneficiaries. Although Bill retained the right to change the beneficiaries until his death, this meant only that the trust was revocable during life and became irrevocable on Bill's death.

If no valid express trust were found to exist, Tom and his wife should nevertheless be able to persuade the court to impose a *constructive* trust upon two-thirds of the insurance proceeds. The constructive trust doctrine creates an equitable duty to convey property to another when retention of the property will unjustly enrich the holder at the expense of others who are entitled to benefit. Because Joe told Bill that he would do whatever Bill requested (upon which statement Bill presumably relied), Joe would be unjustly enriched if he were to retain more than one-third of the insurance proceeds.

Blackacre (the "Farm"):

The circumstances surrounding delivery of the deed to Pete raise several preliminary questions:

Was the deed "delivered"?

Nothing in the facts suggest that there was any defect in the execution of the deed. But before a deed is deemed to transfer title, it must not only be properly executed; it must also be "delivered." The requirement of delivery does not mean that the grantor must hand the deed physically to the grantee. The delivery requirement is satisfied by "words or conduct of the grantor which evidence his intention to make his deed presently operative...so as to vest title in the grantee and to surrender his own control over the title..." 3 A.L.P. 312. In other words, the requirement revolves around intent to convey rather than any specific physical act.

Here, there is concrete evidence of Bill's intent to convey to Pete. He went to Pete's house for the specific purpose of handing Pete the deed. He left the deed with Pete's housekeeper with instructions to deliver it to Pete. He confirmed the status of Pete as title holder by giving him instructions in his signed letter about the disposition of rental income. The delivery is not qualified by the fact that the deed was handed to the housekeeper instead of Pete himself. Bill regarded her only as a conduit to Pete, not as a stakeholder or escrowee.

Acceptance by Pete

Some courts hold that a deed does not convey title until there is some manifestation of acceptance by the grantee. It may be argued that Pete could not have accepted the deed because he did not receive it until his return, which followed Bill's death. However, Pete had previously received and read Bill's letter directing him to collect the rents from the farm and to pay the income to June. If he had wished to reject the conveyance, he would presumably have notified Bill of the rejection before he left on his trip.

Was the deed a testamentary transfer which failed to qualify as a will?

June may wish to argue that the transfer of title to Pete was ineffective because the deed was not accepted by Pete until after Bill's death and therefore constituted a testamentary document which did not meet the requirements for a valid will. The consequence would be that title did not pass under the deed but would instead go to June under the will. This argument is not likely to succeed under the facts. When Bill executed the deed, he had no reason to contemplate an imminent death. His execution of the deed and his letter to Pete indicated an immediate intention to convey title to Pete. Pete read the letter and knew its terms. He never rejected the terms. Bill made a deliberate effort to deliver the will. None of these circumstances indicates any intent on Bill's part to consider this a transfer which would take effect only on his death.

Did the deed to Pete create an inter vivos trust?

Finally, we ask whether the transfer to Pete created an inter vivos trust of income for June during her life, then the fee to Bill's church. Did Bill make the required "manifestation of an intent" to create a trust? Bill executed the deed first, *then* wrote and signed the "trust letter." Pete will argue that he is not bound to observe the trust. He will contend that the deed conveyed unrestricted title to him alone, without any reference to any trust. He will also argue that the letter to him did not meet the formal requirements for creating a trust: it was not executed prior to or at the same time as the deed, and it was not agreed to in writing by Pete as trustee.

June will argue in response that most courts allow the settlor's intent to create a trust to be shown by acts or words occurring *after* the conveyance. Bill's act of writing and mailing the letter to Pete should serve as proof of his intent to create a trust. She will also argue that Pete's acceptance of the trust and of his responsibility as trustee is proved by his failure to object to the contents of the letter.

In summary, it is likely that the court will find both that the conveyance to Pete was effective and that Bill created a a valid inter vivos trust of the income from the farm for the benefit of June.

Did the reference to Aunt Selma in the will create a testamentary trust?

Aunt Selma may contend that the language in Bill's will referring to her created a trust under which June was obliged to supply Selma's needs for life. June can probably overcome this contention by arguing that Bill's language was merely precatory in nature (it was a mere request, not a clear directive). This argument is supported by Bill's use of the word "recommend" and the request to June to do only as she thought best.

There is no indication that Bill had supported Selma during his lifetime and the language in the will is too weak to support a finding that a trust was intended. The court will probably decide that June is *not* obliged to provide any support to Selma, but may do so if she wishes.

Answer to Question 6

Is Daniel's will valid?

Does the fact that John, a beneficiary, acted as witness render Daniel's will ineffective? The answer is "no." The fact that John was an interested witness would not cause the will to fail. Nor would it cause the provision in favor of John to fail (UPC § 2-505(b)). The facts do not suggest any undue influence by John on Daniel, and it's only natural to bestow a testamentary gift upon one's brother.

Bequest to Alice:

As residual beneficiary, Bill might be expected to challenge the specific bequests. He will contend that the $5,000 bequest to Alice was revoked by Daniel's cancellation (*i.e.*, drawing a line through it with the intent to revoke it), and (2) that it is not effectively replaced by the $50,000 bequest, which fails because it does not comply with the necessary testamentary formalities (*e.g.*, witnesses). *See*, UPC § 2-507; § 2-502.

Holographic will:

In rebuttal, Alice will argue that the handwritten modification was valid as a holographic will. The statutes controlling holographic wills vary widely from state to state. Some states require that the entire document be in the testator's handwriting, including a full signature. Those states which follow the reasoning of the UPC are much more liberal. They permit as holographic wills writings which bear the handwritten signature of the testator if "material portions" of the document are also in his handwriting. UPC § 2-502(b). Initials will generally suffice as a signature, especially if it's clear that they're in the testator's hand. Bill will argue that the mere insertion of a new number by the testator does not satisfy the "material portions" requirement. Whether the handwritten elements represent a "material portion" can be established by extrinsic evidence. UPC § 2-502(c). Here, the fact that the initials and the altered amount are both in Daniel's hand is probably sufficient to validate the changes.

Testamentary Intention:

Even if the court is reluctant to find a holographic will, Alice has a good chance of getting the court to overlook the need for testamentary formalities, under a new provision which was added to the UPC in 1990. Under new UPC § 2-503, the lack of formalities will be treated as harmless by the court if there is "clear and convincing evidence" that the document at issue (or an addition or alteration to the document) was intended as the decedent's will. Here, the line through the old amount, the handwritten new amount and the initials alongside the new amount, taken together, would probably satisfy this standard. Alice should be entitled to the increased amount.

Doctrine of dependent relative revocation:

Bill's best argument is that Alice should take nothing: 1) the handwritten changes are ineffective; 2) the original bequest to Alice is not restored because Daniel put a line through it, thereby revoking it. In response to these arguments, Alice will at least attempt to rescue the original $5,000 bequest by arguing that the doctrine of dependent relative revocation applies. This doctrine permits a mistaken revocation to be nullified. Under the doctrine, when a testator revokes a will, or a provision in a will, and substitutes a new will or provision under the mistaken belief that the new will or provision is valid, the revocation is viewed as having been conditional or "dependent" upon the validity of the new will or provision. Applying this principle, if Daniel's changes are not valid, the earlier bequest of $5,000 is restored. Daniel obviously would prefer that Alice get $50,000, but if that change is invalid, the $5,000 gift should certainly be revived. If Alice loses on the "holographic will" and "testamentary intent" arguments, she will almost certainly be permitted to receive the original $5,000 gift under the doctrine of dependent relative revocation.

Pretermitted child:

Alice will *not* be able to claim as a pretermitted child (UPC § 2-302). Because Alice was alive when the will was made, she would not be entitled to an intestate share.

Possible trust in favor of Karen:

Karen will contend that the bequest to Bill was subject to a trust for her benefit; that Bill was obligated to provide for her needs. This contention is supported by the fact that Daniel had helped Karen to meet her living expenses during his life, and presumably, would want Karen to be cared for in a similar manner after his death. But Bill is likely to convince the court that Daniel's instructions were only precatory ("it is my *wish* . . ."), and that his bequest is free of the trust.

Is Lois entitled to John's $10,000?

The law distinguishes between a beneficiary who receives property under a promise to convey to another but who changes his mind *after* the testator's death and one who receives property under a similar promise but who never intended to keep the promise in the first place, or who did intend to keep his promise but changed his mind *before* the testator's death. In the former case, the beneficiary is generally allowed to keep the property free of the promise. In the latter case, a constructive trust is generally applied in favor of the person who will benefit from the promise.

Lois will contend that she is entitled to the $10,000 which Daniel left to John, on the theory that a constructive trust arose because Daniel relied on John's promise to convey the money to Lois, even though the promise was oral. Where there is adequate extrinsic evidence of the testator's reliance upon the beneficiary's promise, most courts will impose a *constructive trust* in favor of the intended beneficiary. As we've pointed out, the court is more likely to do this if it believes that John never intended to keep the promise--or that he did intend to keep the promise but changed his mind before the testator's death--than if it believes he originally intended to comply and changed his mind after the testator's death. We don't know from these facts what John's state of mind was, nor are we told that John has manifested an intent not to convey to Lois. If there is a dispute between them, Lois is likely to prevail.

Summary:

Probably, Alice will receive $50,000, either Lois or John will receive $10,000, and Bill will receive $40,000 without any obligation to care for Karen.

Answer to Question 7

Beneficiaries of Trust #2 ("Beneficiaries") v. Agatha

A testamentary trustee derives her authority both from her designation under the will and her appointment by the court. Once appointed, the trustee owes a duty of loyalty to the beneficiaries of the trust. She may not, for example, sell any trust property to herself without the approval of the court regardless of the fairness or good faith of the transaction. The duty of loyalty precludes the trustee from making any personal profit from trust transactions. When the duty of loyalty is breached, beneficiaries can recover from the trustee: 1) any loss resulting from the breach; 2) any profit resulting from the breach; and 3) any profit the trust would have made if the breach had not occurred. The beneficiaries have several equitable remedies as well (*e.g.*, an injunction to prevent the trustee's breach; an action to appoint a receiver; an action to compel a waiver of the trustee's compensation). In addition, when trust property is wrongfully transferred to a third party, the beneficiaries may trace the property and/or its product into the hands of the third party and secure its return to the trust.

There is little doubt on these facts that Agatha breached her duty of loyalty by utilizing trust property to satisfy a personal obligation. Her actions resulted in a substantial loss to the Beneficiaries. She is therefore liable to the Beneficiaries for at least the loss in the TT & A stock's value to Trust #2 at the time of transfer ($11,000). In most states, she will also be liable for any increase in the stock's value *to the time of trial* (plus any lost dividends).

Beneficiaries of Trust #2 ("Beneficiaries") v. Larry

If the Beneficiaries believe that TT & A stock will continue to increase in value, they can seek to trace the stock and recover the shares directly from Larry.

Under the constructive trust doctrine, when the retention of identifiable property would result in unjust enrichment to the recipient at the expense of the intended beneficiary, the court may deem the item to be held in trust for the benefit of the intended beneficiary. The Beneficiaries will contend that, because Larry received the stock as a gift, the constructive trust doctrine should be applied to require him to return the stock to them.

Larry will respond that he received the stock from his uncle John, a *bona fide* purchaser for value and that he stands in John's shoes. But this argument will probably fail because John did not act in good faith. He knew or should have known: 1) that Agatha was transferring trust assets; and 2) that the assets were worth much more than he paid for them, *i.e.*, enough to enable Agatha to pay off her entire loan balance, plus 10% interest. Equity requires that the Beneficiaries prevail against Larry.

If the TT & A stock is recovered by the Beneficiaries, can John invade Trust #1 to satisfy Agatha's obligation to him? If the Beneficiaries obtain a judgment against Agatha, can they invade Trust #1?

If Larry is forced to return the stock to the trust, John will probably stop at nothing in a renewed effort to recover Agatha's $10,000 from the assets of Trust #1. He will argue there has been a material failure of consideration and that he released Agatha from her obligation without receiving anything in return. The question is: can John invade Trust #1 to satisfy his $10,000 debt?

Ordinarily, a trust beneficiary may assign or transfer her interest in the same way as a fee owner. When the testator wishes to prevent unlimited transfer by the beneficiary, he may use one of several restraints. One of these is a spendthrift trust. A spendthrift trust is one which includes an express provision prohibiting alienation of a beneficiary's right to receive a benefit, whether principal or interest or both. The provision may be limited to voluntary transfers, but it may also be written to apply to involuntary transfers. A majority of states enforce spendthrift provisions; a minority do not.

Most spendthrift clauses express two restraints: (1) a restraint which prevents the beneficiary from voluntarily alienating her interest in the trust income or corpus, and (2) a restraint which prevents creditors of the beneficiary from reaching the interest of the beneficiary. Most courts which enforce spendthrift clauses will construe a will which contains either restraint as intending both. These courts hold that it is against public policy to permit a settlor to restrain involuntary alienation without also restraining voluntary alienation. Some courts will not enforce a restraint against involuntary transfer unless there is also a restraint against voluntary transfer. These courts permit creditors to reach the beneficiary's interest if the beneficiary is not also restrained.

Both of George's trusts stated that "creditors could not reach the income in the trustee's hands." We may reasonably conclude that there was no corresponding provision specifically enjoining voluntary alienation by the beneficiaries. In those states in which a spendthrift provision will not be enforced without such a clause, Agatha's creditors can invade the trust (at least to the extent of her income interest).

In the majority of states, however, the restraint against creditors will be construed as including a restraint against voluntary alienation as well. In those states, John will be prevented from reaching Agatha's interest.

John may have one final ace up his sleeve. The general rule is a settlor may not create a trust for himself. John will argue that the agreement between George and Agatha was a skillful effort to avoid this rule.

John will argue that Agatha really acted as settlor of her own trust by forgiving the $300,000 debt to George's estate and agreeing to substitute the trust instead. He may be able to prove that the arrangement between Agatha and George was a ruse to limit access to Agatha's assets by her creditors.

The same arguments made by John will be made by Agatha's other creditors, including the beneficiaries of Trust #2.

Answer to Question 8

Was a valid trust created thirty years ago?

Four elements must combine to create a valid trust: 1) intent to create the trust; 2) delivery to a trustee (unless the trustor declares himself to be trustee); 3) an identifiable trust res; and 4) a named beneficiary, or, at least, one described sufficiently to permit his identification within the period of the Rule Against Perpetuities. The facts here state that a trust instrument was executed, that State Bank was named trustee, and that 80 shares of Disney stock were delivered to the trustee. Thus, the first three elements of a valid trust are in place.

However, because Thea had no children "in being" at the time the trust was created, it may be argued that the fourth requirement fails because there is no living person who may be identified as the beneficiary and therefore no person to ensure the enforceability of the trust. Trusts for unborn children are valid if there is one beneficiary in existence when the trust is created who is able to enforce the trust.

Here, there is no living beneficiary but it's possible that a beneficiary will be born thereafter, especially since Thea is already pregnant. Under these circumstances, the decisive factor is this: was the trust created by a transfer in trust or by a declaration of trust. If the former, the trust is valid. The trustee is considered a resulting trustee for the benefit of the settlor (Thea), who may enforce the trust until a child is born.

If the latter is true (the trust is created by a declaration of trust), then the courts are split. Some courts hold that no trust is created because there's no one to enforce it; some hold that the trust is valid so long as the interest must vest in a child within the period of the Rule Against Perpetuities.

Here, Thea's trust was created by the transfer of Disney stock to the Bank as trustee under a trust agreement. The trust is valid.

Did the bequest to Fred in Thea's will revoke the trust?

Sal might contend that the gift of 100 shares to Fred revoked the *inter vivos* trust, on the theory that the "out of shares held by me" language implied that Thea owned more than 100 shares and that only some of her shares would be taken "out of" the total to satisfy the gift to Fred. Because this would be true only if we included the shares in the trust, Thea meant to revoke the trust. But the children are likely to prevail against this argument. They will contend: (1) in most states, an *inter vivos* trust cannot be revoked unless the power to revoke is expressly retained by the settlor, and (2) even if the power to revoke was specifically reserved in the trust document (the facts are silent on this point), revocation of a trust must be clear and unequivocal. The will stated that Fred was to receive the stock "out of shares held by me at my death." Most likely, Thea anticipated the acquisition of more shares of Disney stock prior to her death, but intended nothing more by this language. Furthermore, the will contained no reference to the trust agreement, and we are not told that Thea made any effort to reclaim the Disney stock from State Bank. It's unlikely that the court will decide that the trust agreement was revoked.

To whom should the trust assets be distributed?

When the term "children" is used in a trust document or will, it is generally construed as including only the generation immediately following the trustor or testator (*i.e.*, it does *not* include grandchildren). If this view is followed, Thea's one surviving grandchild would receive nothing.

Under the UPC, however, if a will includes a devise in the form of a class gift (to "my children"), a substitute gift is created in the surviving descendants of a deceased member of the class who would have been a beneficiary if he had survived, provided that the deceased class member is a descendant of the testator. (UPC § 2-603(b)(2)). Under this section, descendants of a deceased beneficiary take in the beneficiary's place (by right of representation). Though the UPC provision applies to testamentary gifts and not to *inter vivos* trusts, a court might be persuaded to apply it by analogy. In that event, Thea's two children and her grandchild would each receive one-third of the 200 shares held in trust.

What is the effect of Thea's divorce from Fred?

The UPC provides that the dissolution of a marriage has the effect of revoking a testamentary gift to the former spouse (UPC § 2-804(b)), unless the will or a court order or a marital agreement expressly provides to the contrary. Therefore, Fred gets nothing. (This would be so even if there were no codicil or the codicil were, for some reason, invalidated.)

What does Sal receive?

When a stock dividend by a corporation results in an increase in the number of its securities bequeathed by a testator at the execution of her will, the increase is added to the original bequest, whether the bequest was specific or general (UPC § 2-605(a)(1)). Therefore, Sal is entitled to the 50-share increase that occurred between the time the codicil was executed and the testator's death. His gift includes the 100 shares allocated to him in the will, plus the additional fifty shares issued as a stock dividend before Thea's death.

What is the effect of the stock dividend which occurred after Thea's death?

Because all interests in the estate became vested at Thea's death, the stock dividend during the period of administration will pass to Sal.

Answer to Question 9

1. How should Alice's estate be distributed?

Does it matter that Daniel was not mentioned in the will?

In general, a testator is free to disinherit a child in his will. Some states have attempted to mitigate the effect of this general principle. Thus, some states bar a child only if the intent to disinherit is expressed in the will. In some states, the statute protects only children born after the will is executed. The UPC now protects after-born children only, in circumstances which are not relevant under these facts. UPC § 2-302. But the UPC makes no provision for a child who is alive at the execution of the will unless the testator erroneously believes that child to be dead (in which case the child is treated as an omitted after-born child). Daniel's arguments will fall on deaf ears. Alice made adequate provision for Daniel both in the original trust and also by adding to the trust in her will. There is no reason to conclude that she meant to do anything more for Daniel.

Should the $100,000 bequest to the trustee fail?

According to the facts, Daniel has asserted that the $100,000 bequest to Bank as trustee should fail because the trust document was not executed in compliance with the Statute of Wills. This argument will also fail.

There is nothing in the facts to suggest that the original trust instrument was defective in any way or that it was invalid. The bequest to Bank will simply operate as a gift to an existing valid legal entity. The doctrine of incorporation by reference permits a separate writing which is in existence when a will is made to be incorporated within the will, if the language of the will (1) manifests an intent to incorporate the document, and (2) describes the document sufficiently to permit its identification. Although the doctrine is generally applied to informal documents of the testator which he wants to include within his will, it can be applied by extension here. The trust agreement (including the amendment signed by Daniel himself) was already in existence when the will was executed, And it was specifically mentioned in the will.

Did the bequest to Celia lapse at her death?

A will is deemed effective as of the date of the testator's death. A gift to a named beneficiary who has died before the testator is therefore deemed invalid. It is said to lapse. Most states have statutes which control the disposition of a lapse bequest. Under the UPC's anti-lapse provision, when a beneficiary who is a lineal descendant of the testator's grandparent predeceases the decedent, the gift passes to her surviving descendants. (UPC § 2-603(b)(1)). As Alice's sister, Celia was protected by this provision. Doris is entitled to receive the $50,000 devise to Celia as Celia's sole surviving descendant.

Is Doris' claim affected by her witnessing of the will?

At common law, any person having a pecuniary interest in the testator's estate was incompetent to act as witness to the testator's will. This impediment has been changed by statute in most states. Under the UPC, "...Interest no longer disqualifies a person as a witness, nor does it invalidate or forfeit a gift under the will." (UPC § 2-505, Official Comment). Furthermore, Doris did not have a pecuniary interest at the time she signed the will. Celia was still alive to take the gift and Doris was not an "interested person" as that term is defined in the UPC. (UPC § 1-201(24)).

Conclusion:

Based upon the foregoing, (1) Bank, in its capacity as trustee of the trust established by Alice, would receive $100,000 from her estate, (2) Doris would receive $50,000, and (3) the balance would pass to Stan.

2. Can Phil reach Celia's interest in the trust?

In his attempts to reach Celia's assets in the trust, Phil has probably asserted that the spendthrift provisions added to the trust were invalid against him as a pre-existing creditor of Celia.

Phil might have initially have argued that an *inter vivos* trust cannot ordinarily be terminated or modified by the settlor, unless this power has been specifically retained by her. However, most jurisdictions permit a settlor to terminate or modify an *inter vivos* trust provided the trustee and *all* of the outstanding beneficiaries agree. *See,* Rest. 2d of Trusts, § 338(1). Because Bank, Alice, Celia and Daniel were the trustee, the settlor and all the beneficiaries, they had the power to modify the trust by adding the spendthrift provision.

Phil might make a second, more powerful, argument: that Celia's conduct in securing and participating in the execution of the amendment constituted a *fraud upon Phil as Celia's creditor*. Fraud on creditors occurs when a debtor attempts to place her assets beyond the reach of creditors without giving fair value for the assets or while retaining a concealed interest in the assets. Celia was arguably guilty of such conduct because she entered into a modification of the trust only to insulate her interest from Phil, while preserving her ability to receive income from the trust. When a fraud upon a creditor has occurred, the creditor may invade the trust to the extent of his debtor's interest.

The facts don't tell us whether Celia's consent was in fact necessary to effectuate a modification of the trust, or whether her consent was superfluous because Alice reserved the power to amend in the original instrument. If Celia's consent was crucial to the modification, Phil's "fraud upon creditors" argument should prevail.

However, if Alice had reserved the power to amend the trust without Celia's consent, Phil's contention would be weaker. Even then, however, if it were shown that Celia induced Alice to make the change for the purpose of defeating Phil's rights as creditor, a court might find that Phil had been defrauded.

(Note that the modern trend is to allow certain classes of creditors to reach a beneficiary's interest in a spendthrift trust. Under some statutes a creditor who has rendered personal services to the beneficiary may reach the beneficiary's interest. Phil might be able to persuade the court that his services as building contractor should be included in the definition of personal services. Other creditors who may reach spendthrift trust interests: 1) persons the beneficiary is bound to support; 2) tort claimants; 3) federal and state governments.)

Answer to Question 10

1. Is Tina's will valid in Calco?

Under UPC § 2-506, a will is valid if it was executed in compliance with the law of the place where the will was executed, or with the law of the place where the testator was domiciled or had "an abode" at either the time of the execution or at the time of her death. Thus, while we are told that Tina's will was not valid under the law of Terra, it is valid in Calco — the place of Tina's domicile at death. The facts tell us that Calco's Probate Code is the same as the UPC. Tina's will qualifies as a holographic will (*i.e.*, a will which is signed by the testator and the material terms of which are in the testator's handwriting). *See* UPC § 2-502(b).

Though Sally is an interested person as defined in UPC § 1-201(24), her signature does not invalidate the will. First, a holographic will does not need to be witnessed at all, so Sally's signature was irrelevant to the validity of the will. Secondly, under the UPC, the signing of a will by an interested witness does not invalidate the will or any provision of it. UPC § 2-505(b). Of course, a person opposing the will may be able to show that the witness --especially one who receives a substantial benefit under the will--exerted undue influence on the testator. See Comment, UPC § 2-505.

2. How should Tina's estate be distributed?

Claims on behalf of George:

Can George's guardian claim an interest by George under the "pretermitted child" doctrine? UPC § 2-302 deals with "omitted children." Was George's father Charlie an omitted child of Tina? The answer is "no." The UPC protects an omitted child only if (1) the testator erroneously believed the child, though alive, was deceased, or (2) the child was born or adopted *after* the execution of the will. Charlie was not an omitted child as that term is defined and George cannot claim through him. Further, the protection accorded to omitted children under UPC § 2-302 does not extend to omitted grandchildren. The term "child" specifically excludes grandchildren of a testator. *See* General Definitions, UPC § 1-201(5). A grandchild--even one born or adopted after the will is executed-- cannot avail himself of the omitted child provisions of the UPC. George will receive nothing, even though he is an after-born issue of a child of the testator.

(Note: To enable us to discuss other issues arising under these facts, we'll assume that George is treated as a pretermitted heir.)

Gifts to Sally:

We have determined that Tina's will is valid in Calco. Does Sally's status as witness affect her status as beneficiary under the will? Under UPC § 2-505, the signing of a will by an interested witness does not invalidate either the will or any of its provisions. The provisions for Sally's benefit remain intact. Sally was Tina's daughter and the natural object of Tina's affection and her largesse. Nothing in the facts indicates that Sally exercised any undue influence on her mother. On the contrary, we know that Tina later gave Sally enough money to buy a house.

Which house is "the house" referred to in the will?

George's guardian may contend that Tina meant to give Sally only the house in Terra, and that when the Terra house was sold, the doctrine of ademption by extinction applied and made the gift ineffective. At common law, ademption was applied mechanically; if the property referred to in the will was not in the estate at death, the gift failed. The modern trend is to soften the impact of ademption. One device is to construe the will as though it read at the death of the testator, not at the date of execution. Under this device, the original gift is deemed replaced by any substitute that may exist at death. Another device is to read the disposition in its most general sense instead of as referring to specific property. Thus, "my" house becomes not a specific house, but any building in which the testator resides.

The Uniform Probate Code offers relief in the case of substituted real or tangible personal property. UPC § 2-606(a) provides: "A specific devisee has a right to the specifically devised property in the testator's estate at death and:... (5) real or tangible personal property owned by the testator at death which the testator acquired as a replacement for specifically devised real or tangible personal property;..." Under this provision, the Calco house would be substituted for the Terra house under the will.

Even if the specific bequest fails, the Calco house will still go to Sally under the residuary clause.

The significance of the $300,000 "advancement":

Tina did not use the term "advancement" correctly. The term is applied only in the case of total or partial intestacy. An advancement is an inter vivos transfer made by a deceased before his death to a person who is entitled to take in intestacy, which the testator intended as an advance against the person's final disposition from the intestate estate. Example: A has two sons, B and C. A dies intestate, leaving $100,000 in cash. Two years before his death, A gave son B $50,000 with the admonition, "This is an advance against your money when I die." The total estate is deemed to be $150,000; B gets an additional $25,000 and C gets $75,000. Under the UPC, an inter vivos gift to an heir of an individual who dies intestate is treated as an advancement only if: 1) the testator declares in a contemporaneous writing that the gift is an advancement, or the donee acknowledges it in writing; or 2) a writing of the decedent, or a written acknowledgment of the donee, indicates that the gift is to be taken into account in computing the division and distribution of the intestate estate.

Here, it's clear that by using the word "advancement" Tina meant only that she was giving Sally some money she needed then instead of keeping it for Sally as part of the residue of Tina's estate under her will.

Was the devise of the house to Sally satisfied by the inter vivos gift of $300,000?

When Tina gave $300,000 to Sally for the purchase of a house, did she intend that the gift of cash should "satisfy" --*i.e.*, substitute for--the bequest of the house. The effect of construing the gift as a satisfaction would be to revoke the bequest of the house. At common law, there was authority for the proposition that a substantial inter vivos gift to a child who was also a legatee presumably satisfied the legacy if the other beneficiaries of the will were other children of the testator. The presumption was rebuttable by evidence of a contrary intent by the testator.

Under UPC § 2-609, an inter vivos gift is treated as a satisfaction only if the will provides for deduction, or if the testator declares in writing that the gift is in satisfaction of the devise, or if the devisee acknowleges in writing that the gift is in satisfaction. None of these alternatives has occurred here, and, because Calco's Probate Code follows the UPC, the gift of $300,000 to Sally will not be treated as having satisfied the devise of the house in the will.

Summary:

Sally receives Tina's entire estate.

Answer to Question 11

Has Tippi created a valid charitable trust?

A charitable trust must have six identifiable elements: (1) the settlor's manifested intent to create a trust; (2) a trust res; (3) a trustee to manage the trust; (4) a charitable purpose; (5) a definable class of beneficiaries; and 6) eligibility by all members of the class to receive or share in the benefits. The class of beneficiaries may be very broad (*e.g.*, all the residents of a state or community). If all the other elements are present, a charitable trust is not likely to fail for lack of an ascertainable class of beneficiaries. The public at large is considered to be the beneficiary and the Attorney General of the state may enforce the trust on the public's behalf.

Although Tippi seems not to have used the term "trust" in her documents, she nevertheless (1) signed a declaration of intent designating a class of beneficiaries who would benefit from her gift (*i.e.*, "the inhabitants of the city"); 2) created a charitable purpose (the Tippi Library); 3) designated "trustees" (the three-person Board of Governors); and (4) delivered to the trustees a $100,000 check and a deed conveying the land to be used for the library (the trust res). All the necessary elements of a charitable trust appear to be satisfied

Any function of a governmental or municipal nature, or any activity which is beneficial to the general community, is usually accepted as a "charitable" purpose. Since one of the traditional functions of government or of any organized society is to provide libraries for its citizens, Tippi's purpose is clearly charitable. The trust res consists of the land and the proceeds of Tippi's $100,000 check.

Who gets Tippi's stocks and bonds?

The facts require the court to determine whether Tippi's stocks and bonds pass to the trust or whether the gift to the trust fails for lack of implementation. Tippi's trust was essentially an irrevocable inter vivos trust. To the extent that she manifested an intent to create a charitable trust, designated the trustees of the trust, and transferred substantial property to the trust, she had done all she could to effectuate creation of an enforceable trust. The Board can argue that the provision for installment delivery of Tippi's itemized stocks and bonds was simply a device by her to discipline the Board to budget its expenditures in the construction and maintenance of the library. Under her plan, the Board would receive $250,000 each quarter, a substantial sum which would enable the Board to plan and spend prudently.

The Board will also argue that the court should impose a constructive trust on the stocks and bonds because it was clearly Tippi's intent that the trust should receive them. Only her death prevented her from completing delivery of the first installment. If she had lived long enough to make the first installment, then there would be no question that she intended to complete the others. It would be inequitable to allow Betty to defeat Tippi's manifest intent.

If Betty argued that the trust was admittedly irrevocable as to the $100,000 check and the land but revocable by Tippi before her death as to the stocks and bonds, then the Board can respond that a revocable inter vivos trust which has not in fact been revoked by the testator before her death has testamentary effect. On these facts, that would result in the transfer of the stocks and bonds to the trustees at Tippi's death.

The trustees can also argue that the document containing an itemized list of her stocks and bonds should be incorporated into the trust declaration by reference in the same way as documents extrinsic to a will can be incorporated into the will by reference. The list was executed on the same day as the declaration and was intended to be an integral part of her trust scheme. The entire project would collapse without the additional funds. Tippi would not have transferred land and money to the trustees without intending at the same time to provide the rest of the funds necessary to carry out her intent.

Betty will argue that the document listing the stocks and bonds was not referred to in the declaration exactly because Tippi wanted the gift of stocks and bonds to be revocable by her and that the gift of stocks and bonds was in fact revoked by her death. Her argument is supported by the fact that Tippi had not in fact delivered them to the trustees or executed any document which clearly manifested an intent to transfer them to the Board at her death.

In the absence of additional facts, the court could reasonably decide in favor of either party.

Can the Board use the block of land as a public park and maintain it with the trust funds?

When a charitable trust is created for a particular purpose and the purpose cannot be accomplished, the trust is said to fail. A resulting trust in favor of the settlor is then said to occur. Betty will contend that the trust purpose here (the construction and maintenance of a public library) has failed, and that a resulting trust has occurred for the benefit of Tippi and her estate. On this theory, the Board should be ordered to transfer title to the trust res back to Tippi's estate.

However, the Board will argue that the *cy pres* doctrine should be applied to permit the use of the trust res for a public park. Under this doctrine, when the specific purpose for which a charitable trust has been created cannot be carried out, the court may permit the trust to continue for a *similar* purpose, provided this similar purpose fits within the testator's "general charitable intent." The court attempts to put itself into the testator's mind and decide whether the testator would prefer to support some reasonably comparable charitable purpose or to cause the assets to revert to her heirs.

Betty will contend that Tippi wanted to build only a library and would not have made any gift to the Board if she had known that it would not be used for this purpose. The Board will argue in rebuttal that the deed to the property was "in perpetuity," proving that Tippi intended the Board to keep the land even if some other good purpose had to be substituted.

Because courts ordinarily prefer to validate a charitable trust rather than destroy it, it is likely that the *cy pres* doctrine will be applied. Thus, the Board will probably be allowed to create and maintain the park with the land and funds given to the trust by Tippi, even if the Board doesn't get to use the proceeds of the stocks and bonds.

Answer to Question 12

What is the effect of the divorce upon the gift to Leonard?

Except as may otherwise be provided in a court order, another "governing instrument," or a contract providing for the division of the marital estate, a divorce has the effect of revoking a testamentary gift to the former spouse. Here, there is no property settlement agreement and no evidence of any court order, so Leonard would *not* be entitled to take anything from the estate. (UPC § 2-804(b)). If Fay's estate is not disposed of by the other bequests, the residuary will be disposed of as if Fay had died intestate. If the other bequests exhaust all of Fay's assets, there will be no residue.

The UPC provides that, if the testator dies leaving descendants (but no spouse), the residuary estate passes to the descendants by representation. The estate is divided at the earliest level at which there are living descendants. (UPC § 2-103(1)). This means that, assuming both were alive, Linda and Michael would each receive one-half of the residuary estate. But because Michael is deceased, Roberta, his adopted daughter, would take his half of the residuary estate by representation.

How will the proceeds of the sale of the "business property" be disposed of?

Ademption:

At common law, a *specific* devise of property which was no longer in the testator's estate at her death was usually treated as "adeemed," *i.e.*, cancelled. A specific devise is a gift which is clearly identifiable as against all other assets of the estate. Because the Main Street property was disposed of by Fay many years before her death, ademption would appear to apply, wiping out the gift of this property to Linda.

However, the modern trend is to discourage ademption. Some states have statutes which create the presumption that the testator does not intend ademption if the proceeds of the specific bequest can be followed into other assets of the testator at her death. Some courts interpret the bequest as one of form only; a change in the form of a gift is not relevant if the testator intends one form to replace another.

The current version of UPC § 2-606 confirms the presumption against ademption. It provides that even if the substituted assets are not clearly a replacement for the original bequest (in this case, one business property for another), a specific beneficiary is entitled to the value of any specific bequest, real or personal, to the extent that such property is not in the testator's estate at death, unless it appears that the testator intended ademption. Here, we are told that Fay sold the Main Street business property for $20,000. Under the UPC, Linda is entitled to secure the sum of $20,000 from the estate in lieu of the business property. We're not told whether the business property was a parcel of real estate or simply the business assets of an ongoing retail business within rental property, but, for purposes of our analysis, this doesn't matter.

It's important to note that Linda is entitled to get only $20,000 under this analysis. Because Fay left $25,000 in bank accounts, at least $5,000 of Fay's cash will pass to the residue and be distributed as in intestacy.

Is there a Totten trust for Linda?

One of Fay's cash assets was the $10,000 deposited into a bank account designated "Fay Woods, Trustee for Linda Woods." This will probably be construed as a Totten trust (*i.e.*, the trust relationship is created by the designation upon the savings account). A Totten trust is in the nature of a revocable trust. The trust res is owned by the trustee during her lifetime and may be used or withdrawn by her, but passes to the beneficiary upon the death of the trustee. Thus, Linda should be entitled to the $10,000. But even if the bank account is not valid as a Totten trust, the $10,000 in the account should go to Linda as part of the assets substituted for the Main Street business property.

The money in Fay's commercial account will be divided between Linda and the residue -- $10,000 to Linda to substitute in part for the business property, and $5,000 to the residue.

What disposition should be made of the jewelry described in the typed note?

The note designating the specific jewelry which would pass to Linda was not executed with the requisite testamentary formalities. The execution was not witnessed and therefore, the note does not qualify as a codicil. No part of the note except the signature and date was in the testator's handwriting, so it was not a valid holographic will. But Linda should still be able to convince the court to admit the list as part of the will.

First, under the doctrine of incorporation by reference, material extraneous to the will which was: (1) in existence when the will was created; (2) referred to in the will in a way which shows the testator's intent to incorporate it; and (3) described sufficiently to permit its identification, will become part of the will. (UPC § 2-510). Of course, the UPC does require that the extraneous writing be in existence when the will was executed, and it's not clear from these facts which document came first. However, because they're both dated on the same day and the will refers to jewelry "as is enumerated" on the list, the court will probably presume that the list preceded the will and should be incorporated.

Second, even if the list was not in existence at the time the will was created, it will probably still be incorporated under UPC § 2-513. This provision states that a will may refer to an extraneous written list to dispose of specific items of tangible personal property provided that: (1) the writing is signed by the testator; (2) the items and the devisee of the items are clearly identified; and (3) the items are "tangible personal property not otherwise specifically disposed of by the will, other than money." In addition, UPC § 2-513 provides that "[t]he writing may be referred to as one to be in existence at the time of the testator's death; it may be prepared before or after the execution of the will; it may be altered by the testator after its preparation; and it may be a writing that has no significance apart from its effect on the dispositions made by the will." Since the note in question satisfies all of the requirements, it will be effective to constitute a gift to Linda of the jewelry mentioned in it.

How does Michael's death affect the gift of stock in the will?

Because Michael was a lineal descendant of Fay, the gift of stock to him (which would otherwise lapse because of his failure to survive Fay) will pass to Roberta, his descendant. (UPC § 2-603(b)). Although adopted, Roberta is considered to be a child of both Wanda and Michael. (UPC § 2-114(b)).

How does the stock dividend affect the testamentary gift to Michael?

Under the Uniform Probate Code, the devisee of stock in an organization is entitled to additional securities of the same organization owned by the testator by reason of action initiated by that organization, excluding any resulting from the exercise of stock options (UPC § 2-605). This would include stock dividends. It doesn't matter that some of the securities included in the dividend are of a different class (*e.g.*, Class B) from those that were the direct subject of the bequest — so long as the issuing organization is the same, UPC § 2-605 applies. Thus, both the original stock and the stock dividends would pass to Roberta by reason of the anti-lapse provision.

In summary, Linda gets $20,000 inclusive of the Totten trust, and the jewelry as well. Roberta gets all the XYZ stock. Linda and Roberta share equally in the $5,000 residue.

Answer to Question 13

The impact of Tess' marriage on her 1988 will:

If Tess had not executed any other testamentary documents after she executed the will, her marriage to Hubert would have had a significant impact on her testamentary plans. Under the UPC, a surviving spouse who marries the testator *after* her will is executed is entitled under most circumstances to receive the value of his intestate share of all assets left by the testator, at least, to the extent that the assets are not left to a child of the testator who was born before the marriage. UPC § 2-301. Because it does not appear that Tess had a child before the marriage, Hubert would have been entitled to take his intestate share.

Effect of the 1990 "codicil":

When a testator labels a testamentary document a "codicil" rather than a "will," the normal assumption is that she intends only to alter, amend or clarify a prior will. But when the document — although labelled a "codicil" — completely disposes of the testator's property, it will be strongly presumed that she intended a new will revoking all prior wills, not an amendment. See UPC § 2-507(c). Under this rule of interpretation, the August 4, 1990 document will be presumed to represent a new and complete will, because it completely disposes of Tess' estate. The document satisfies the UPC's holographic will requirements (*i.e.*, the material provisions are in the testator's handwriting, and it is signed by the testator). (UPC § 2-502(b).) The so-called "codicil" became Tess' new will.

Effect of Sonny's birth:

If the 1990 document continued to control Tess' estate, Sonny would have the right to take his intestate share of her estate. Under UPC § 2-302(a)(1), if a testator has no child living at the time she executes the will, an omitted after-born child takes an intestate share, unless the will devises all or substantially all the estate to the omitted child's other parent, provided that parent survives the testator and is entitled to take under the will. Because the 1990 codicil did not give "substantially all" of her estate to Hubert, Sonny would be entitled to an intestate share. However, as we shall see, Tess' second codicil may have the effect of preventing Sonny from receiving his intestate share.

Did the second codicil revoke the first one?

On first reading, the second "codicil" appears to have revoked the August 4, 1990 document. The first sentence of the second codicil states, "I revoke my codicil of August 4, 1990."

If the codicil is construed as revoking the 1990 document, we are left with two options: either 1) Tess is deemed to have died intestate; or 2) the 1988 will is revived. Because nothing in these facts suggests that Tess intended either of these results and it's clear that Tess merely wanted to abort the gift to State University, it's unlikely that the court would construe the second codicil as anything more than an amendatory document. Extrinsic evidence is generally admissible to explain ambiguities in a will or codicil, and the fact that the second codicil resulted from Tess' dissatisfaction with professionalism in college athletics presumably can be proven. As a consequence of the strong desire by most courts to attempt to effectuate a testator's intent and to avoid intestacy, the second codicil will be deemed to have merely modified, *not* revoked, the August 4, 1990 document.

We have assumed in our discussion that the second codicil meets the formal requirements for a testamentary document under the UPC -- even though it was unwitnessed, it's in the testator's handwriting and signed by her, so it's valid as a holographic testament. (UPC § 2-502(b).)

Effect of the second codicil:

If we proceed under the assumption that the second codicil merely modified the first, it will have affected Tess' previous testamentary scheme in two ways.

First, a codicil is usually deemed to republish and reconfirm a prior will to the extent it does not change or modify the prior will. When Tess executed the second codicil, Sonny was already born. As a child in being, he would no longer qualify as a pretermitted child. Presumably, if Tess had intended otherwise, she would have made provision for Sonny in the second codicil. Because she chose not to, and because the second codicil is valid, Sonny will receive nothing from Tess' estate.

Second, the codicil probably effectively revoked the devise to State University. While Tess' statement, "Nothing to athletic factories like State University," does not specify that the gift is revoked, this conclusion is virtually inescapable, especially since Tess clearly expressed the terms of the alternative gift to Harvale. As we've discussed, extrinsic evidence is ordinarily admissible to explain ambiguities in a will or codicil, and proof that Tess was upset with professionalism in college athletics at the time the second codicil was made would be admissible. The second codicil revoked the devise to State University and substituted the Harvale academic scholarship fund for the earlier gift.

What is the effect of Tess' mistake?

State University will contend that the gift to it should not be revoked because Tess was acting on the mistaken assumption that the college was an athletic factory and that Tess would not have revoked her gift if she had known that the University had voted to discontinue all intercollegiate athletic programs. This type of mistake is known as mistake in the inducement, *i.e.*, the testator was prompted to include or exclude a provision because of her mistaken notion about a particular fact. Courts rarely grant relief to correct a supposed mistake in the inducement. They limit their intervention to mistakes which appear on the face of the will itself, and then only when the will indicates what the testator would have done "but for" the mistake. That is not the case here. The remedy for mistake in the inducement is to deny probate of the codicil. This would represent an extreme remedy which the court would be unlikely to adopt on these facts.

Is the gift to Harvale College valid?

At common law, a gift to charity within the period--usually six months-- immediately before the testator's death was invalid under statutes called mortmain statutes. Under such a statute, the gift to Harvale would be invalid. But very few states still have mortmain statutes, and the Uniform Probate Code does not recognize the mortmain concept. The gift to Harvale is valid.

How should H's estate be distributed?

If we assume that the second codicil controls the disposition of Tess' estate, then Harvale College would receive one-fourth of Tess' estate, Hubert would receive one-half, and Martha one-fourth. This is the most likely result.

Answer to Question 14

1. Is the will valid?

Nelly's will should qualify as a holographic will. A holographic will is valid if it is signed by the testator and the material provisions are in her handwriting. Because Nelly's will is written in her own hand and signed by her, it should be probated. The fact that she signed at the bottom of page 1, instead of at the end of the document, should not invalidate the will; there is no requirement in most states, or under the UPC, that the signature be at the end of the document. (See UPC § 2-502, Official Comment.) In any event, the two items that were written on Page 2 (the date and Brad's signature) were not vital to the integrity of the document. The first page was sufficient to constitute a valid holographic will.

2. How should Nelly's estate be distributed?

Brad as interested witness:

Brad's signature as witness on the will will probably not invoke the common law "interested witness" doctrine to invalidate the will. True, he received a bequest under Nelly's will, but his signature was superfluous. No witness is required to support a holographic will. Brad's signature would ordinarily be ignored on the issue of the will's validity. In any case, under the UPC, the "signing of a will by an interested witness does not invalidate the will or any provision of it." (UPC § 2-505(b)).

Was Ann's gift revoked by striking through her name?

Any part or all of a will may be deemed revoked if the testator has performed a revocatory act on the will itself with the intent and purpose to revoke. The rule applies equally to a holographic will and a will which has been executed before witnesses. The revocatory act may consists of "burning, tearing, canceling, obliterating, or destroying" the will or any part of it. (See UPC § 2-507(a)(1).) If a revocatory act appears on the will, the testator's intent can be proven by extrinsic evidence. The problem is that Brad will not be a disinterested witness in the will contest. It's impossible to tell from the facts who struck the lines through Ann's name. Brad will testify either that Nelly did it herself or that he did it "in the testatator's conscience presence and by the testator's direction." (id.) Ann may respond that the strike-through was done by Brad without Nelly's knowledge and solely to deprive Ann of her share. On these facts, there is no way of telling who would or should be successful.

Lapse of Charlie's share:

When a devisee fails to survive the testator, his devise is said to lapse or fail. Because Charlie predeceased Nelly, his $10,000 gift will lapse. A devise is said to lapse when the beneficiary dies before the testator and the will fails to provide an alternative disposition of the property. Most states and the UPC have adopted anti-lapse provisions to protect certain devisees. If the devise is to a child of the testator who predeceases the testator, his surviving issue will take the devise in his place. UPC § 2-603. Because Charlie had no descendants, there is no one to take his share under the anti-lapse provision.

The stocks and bonds:

A secret trust arises when a bequest in a will appears unconditional and unequivocal but was made upon the oral promise of the devisee to hold the devise in trust for someone else. No reference to the trust is made in the will. In a semi-secret trust, the will makes reference to the existence of a trust but no beneficiary of the trust is specified. Presumably, the testator and the devisee have agreed orally who is to be benefit from the trust. Here, because the language in Nelly's will directed Brad to use the stocks and bonds "as we have agreed," the arrangement would be viewed as a "semi-secret" trust. The majority view under these facts is that the trust fails for lack of a designated beneficiary. Under these circumstances, the named trustee (*i.e.*, Brad) holds the stocks and bonds in a resulting trust for the benefit of the residuary beneficiaries. If there is no residuary clause, they go to the testator's heirs as in intestacy. In a few jurisdictions, a constructive trust is imposed in favor of the intended beneficiary. (*See,* Rest. 2d of Trusts, § 55, Comment h, applying the minority approach.)

If the majority view is followed, the stocks and bonds here will pass by intestacy because there is no residuary clause. If the minority view is accepted, the trust will be enforced according to its (secret) terms. Thus under the minority view, if Brad's testimony is believed, he will take outright (he is the remainderman after the life estate to Charlie), and if his testimony is *not* believed, the gift will fail and pass by intestacy.

The house and Nelly's other personal effects:

When a testator fails to dispose of some of her property by an existing valid will, the property passes by intestacy. On these facts, the house and other personal effects would be shared equally by Brad and Ann. If the semi-secret trust of Nelly's stock and bonds is deemed to fail (see above), then the stock and bonds will also pass to both by intestacy.

If we assume for the purpose of argument that Nelly herself struck through Ann's name and that the specific bequest to Ann was therefore invalid, does this also mean that Ann will be completely disinherited, i.e., that she will not even receive her intestate share? Under the UPC, the testator may disinherit anyone, including a child, but she must do so "expressly." See UPC § 2-101(b). It is unlikely that a court would find that by striking through Ann's name in a clause providing for a specific bequest of a limited amount, Nelly intended to disinherit Ann entirely. It's likely that Ann will be permitted to take her 1/2 intestate share along with Brad, whose testimony is likely to be discounted.

Answer to Question 15

1. Theories upon which Sam may participate in the distribution of Carol's estate.

As pretermitted or omitted child: Under the UPC, when a testator fails to provide for a child because she mistakenly believes that the child is dead, the child is entitled to a share of the estate as a pretermitted or omitted child. (UPC § 2-302(c)). Carol had no reason to doubt that Sam was dead. She had the Army's letter and she confirmed her belief in his death by stating in the will, "In view of the death of my son, Sam . . ." If a testator had one or more children living when she executed her will and the will devised property to one or more of those children, then a pretermitted or omitted child is entitled to a pro-rata share of the gifts to such child or children. (UPC § 2-302(a)(2)). Therefore, Sam takes one-half of the portion of the estate given to his sister, Dot (*i.e.*, one-half of two-thirds of the estate, or one-third of the total).

Constructive trust: The general rule is that anyone deprived of a benefit under a will because of fraud or duress can obtain relief by asking the court to invalidate the entire will or that part of the will which affects him. This general principle is incorporated in UPC § 1-106. That section enables any person injured by fraud in connection with a will to obtain "appropriate relief against the preperator of the fraud or restitution from any person (other than a bone fide purchaser) benefitting from the fraud, whether innocent or not." On these facts, Sam is clearly entitled to recover his half of the assets remaining after the bequests to Tom and Jane, and, possibly, damages against Dot. Most courts under these facts will impose a constructive trust in favor of Sam upon Dot's share. Because Dot fraudulently concealed the Army's letter raising doubts about Sam's death (as a result of which concealment Carol did not make provision for Sam), a constructive trust in favor of Sam should be imposed upon Dot's share. Dot will argue that the letter did not confirm that Sam was alive and that even if Carol had seen the letter, she might not have changed her will until his return was confirmed. But this argument will probably fail. On these facts, the court is not likely to be sympathetic to Dot.

Mistake: If a testator includes or omits a particular bequest because of a mistake in a material fact, the courts are loath to invalidate the will, even though the will may not represent the testator's true intent. (Example: the testator intentionally omits a bequest to his nephew because he believes the nephew has dropped out of law school; in fact, the nephew has graduated with honors.) A mistake of this kind is called a mistake in the inducement. Generally, it will not impede probate of the will. The reason the courts are reluctant to refuse probate: if the will is refused, the estate will be distributed as in intestacy. This is not likely to be the testator's wish. In the limited case in which the testator fails to include a child in the belief the child is dead, the UPC ignores the usual rule regarding mistakes in the inducement and allows the pretermitted or omitted child to share pro rata in any gift made to his siblings. (*See*, discussion of UPC § 2-302(a)(2), *supra*.)

2. Other relief to which Sam may be entitled:

Sam may be able to assert claims against Dot individually, for (1) fraud, (2) interference with a prospective economic advantage, and (3) intentional infliction of severe emotional distress.

Sam can contend that Dot's deceit in withholding the letter was deliberately intended to deprive him of his inheritance. Dot knew that it would cause Sam emotional distress to learn he had been disinherited by his mother, especially when he realized that his mother had continued to suffer under the illusion that he was dead. If Sam is successful on any of these theories, he may be able to recover punitive damages from Dot, in addition to his actual losses.

3. How should Carol's estate be distributed?

Although Carol characterized the *inter vivos* gifts to Tom and Jane as "advancements," she probably intended such gifts to constitute partial "satisfactions" of their testamentary gifts. ("Advancements" pertain to *inter vivos* satisfactions of a beneficiary's *intestate* share of the decedent's estate.)

Jane and Tom could contend that, since the statements made in the ledger were *not* accompanied by the requisite testamentary formalities (*i.e.*, they were not embodied in a formal or holographic will), they are not admissible.

Sam and Dot could argue in rebuttal, however, that UPC § 2-609 provides that a satisfaction occurs where either: (1) the will provides for deduction of an *inter vivos* gift, (2) the testator declares in a contemporaneous writing that the *inter vivos* gift is to be deducted from a testamentary gift, or (3) the devisee acknowledges in writing that the gift is in satisfaction of the devise or that its value is to be deducted from the value of the devise. Since Carol's will referred to the possibility of *inter vivos* satisfactions (the first test above), the court will almost certainly treat the gifts to Jane and Tom as partial satisfactions. (The ledger, though it reverses the numbers, would probably satisfy test (2) above, making it even more likely that the court would find the gifts to have been partial satisfactions.)

Tom might contend that extrinsic evidence is not permissible to vary the plain meaning of a will; and therefore, proof of the erroneous transposition in the ledger may not be offered. However, Jane could successfully argue in rebuttal that extrinsic proof is ordinarily admissible to show a mistake in transcription. Thus, Jane should prevail and be permitted to prove Carol's mistake. In that event, the court will deduct $5,000 from Jane's share and $10,000 from Tom's, as partial satisfactions.

Summary:

If Sam is a pretermitted heir, he would be entitled to one-half of two-thirds of Carol's estate, or $95,000. (The total estate, $285,000, consists of the present estate of $270,000 plus the $15,000 *inter vivos* partial satisfactions.) Dot would be entitled to the other half, $95,000. Jane and Tom would divide the remaining cash, $80,000, in a manner resulting in Jane's receiving $5,000 more than Tom, *i.e.*, $42,500 for Jane and $37,500 for Tom.

If the constructive trust doctrine were applied, Dot would receive two-thirds of $285,000 ($190,000). However, a constructive trust in favor of Sam equal to one-half of that would be imposed upon the devise to Dot. Jane and Tom would divide the remainder, $80,000, as follows: $42,500 for Jane and $37,500 for Tom.

Answer to Question 16

Was the document which Tate signed on December 2, 1997 a valid will?

Although the document prepared by Tate's lawyer in 1997 did not use or mention the word "will," it would appear to have been intended as Tate's will. This is evidenced by the following facts: (1) the document used the words, "I...dispose of all my estate as follows...," and the words, "...I have intentionally omitted all my other heirs;" (2) it disposed of Tate's entire estate; (3) it was prepared at Tate's request by an attorney; and (4) Tate declared it to be his "will" when he withdrew it from his pocket during the party.

Tate's son Art will contend that Tate did not have the requisite testamentary intent when he signed the document at the party. Tate was slightly intoxicated when he signed the document and asked Sally and two of her guests to act as witnesses. Sally will argue that Tate displayed sufficient testamentary intent: (1) he characterized the document as his "will"; (2) he had the presence of mind to have it witnessed; and (3) he later referred to it as a will when he tried to cancel it (discussed below). The requisite testamentary intent would appear to be present.

The fact that Sally was one of the witnesses to the will is not significant. Interested persons (*i.e.*, those receiving a bequest under the will) qualify as witnesses (UPC § 2-505(b)). Besides, since only two witnesses are needed under the UPC (UPC § 2-502(a)(3)), Sally's signature as a third witness would be superfluous.

In summary, Tate would appear to have executed a valid will on December 2, 1997.

Was the typed document which Tate signed on January 20, 1998 a valid will?

Art and Sally will both contend that the document which Tate signed in his lawyer's office on January 20, 1998 was not intended to serve as a codicil to Tate's will, but only as a non-binding memorandum which the lawyer would reduce to a more formal document that Tate would execute at a later date. There is no indication that the January 20, 1998 document was properly witnessed. Tate was in his lawyer's office when the memo was prepared and signed. If he had intended the memo to constitute his will, witnesses were available (the lawyer and his secretary were there). The memo did not satisfy the requirement of UPC § 2-502 that two witnesses sign the will.

Nor could the January 20, 1998 memorandum be probated as a holographic will. The "material provisions" were not in Tate's handwriting. (UPC § 2-502(b)).

An argument can be made that the January 20, 1998 memorandum should be treated as a valid will under UPC § 2-503. This section allows a document not satisfying the formalities for a will to be treated as one, "if the proponent . . . establishes by clear and convincing evidence that the decedent intended the document . . . to constitute . . . the decedent's will. . . ." On these facts, CCF could argue that the handwritten statement written by Tate across the December 1997 will ("I have made a new will") shows that he intended the January 20, 1998 document to be his will. However, it's unlikely that this argument will be enough to meet the "clear and convincing evidence" standard of UPC § 2-503.

We conclude that the January 20, 1998 memorandum probably did not constitute a valid will. It therefore did *not* revoke the December 1997 document under the doctrine of inconsistency. (UPC § 2-507(a)(1)).

Did Tate revoke the December 1997 will by the statement he wrote across it?

Art will contend that the December 1997 will was revoked by two independent means. He will argue first that the words Tate wrote across the will constituted a valid holographic revocation which incorporated the will by reference. An express revocation can be accomplished by utilizing the steps necessary to make a valid holographic will: *i.e.*, the material terms must be in the testator's handwriting, and the document must be signed by the testator. Since the revocation was in Tate's handwriting and was initialed by him (the initials "TT" are sufficient to count as a "signature" — *see,* UPC § 2-502, Comment), these requirements were satisfied.

Art will also argue that the statement written on the will was a valid "revocatory act." UPC § 2-507(a)(2) defines "revocatory act" to include a "canceling" of the will. Cancellation is effective "whether or not the . . . cancellation touched any of the words on the will." The statement here qualifies under this section, and it served to revoke the will.

Art's argument that the December 1997 will was revoked by Tate before his death will probably succeed.

Was the December 1997 document revived by the doctrine of dependent relative revocation ("DDRR")"

The doctrine of DDRR comes into play when the testator attempts to revoke an earlier will by executing a second will and the second will is declared invalid. Under these circumstances, the courts will often presume that the testator would have wished the earlier will to be reinstated if he had known the second will would be ineffective. Unless clear evidence is presented that the testator did not intend this result, the first will will be reinstated. As an extension of her argument that the attempted cancellation of the December 1997 will by Tate's handwritten statement across the face of the will was ineffective, Sally will contend that DDRR should be applied here. She will argue that the cancellation was not valid and that the December 1997 will is revived. She will contend that Tate would not have wanted to die intestate but would clearly have preferred her and her son to Art, whom he had intentionally omitted from the December 1997 will.

Because Art would be the sole recipient of Tate's estate if Tate were deemed to have died intestate, Art would contend that DDRR should *not* be applied. There is no reason to believe that Tate would have wanted the initial will revived — the January 20, 1998 memorandum contained a completely different dispository scheme, and the facts do not show that Tate would have preferred his original scheme over intestacy.

Sally would argue in rebuttal that Tate would have preferred that his estate be distributed in accordance with the December 1997 will rather than according to an arbitrary state-drafted intestacy scheme.

The court would probably be unlikely to apply the doctrine of DDRR on these facts in any event.

Under all the facts, Tate will be deemed to have died intestate. His son Art will inherit Tate's entire estate. UPC § 2-103(1) gives the entire estate of one who dies without a spouse to the testator's "descendants" — and Art is T's only descendant.

Assume Tate's December 1997 will was deemed revived under DDRR. How would his estate be distributed?

For purposes of discussion, two questions arise if the December 1997 will is deemed revived. First question: Was Art alive when the will was made? If he was, then he would receive nothing. But if he was born after Tate made the December 1997 will, he would be considered a pretermitted child and he would receive his intestate share (the entire estate). (UPC § 2-302).

Second question: What was the consequence of Tate's mistake in describing his nephew as "Ron" instead of "Don"? Because (1) Tate has no nephew named "Ron," and (2) the description of the recipient in the will is otherwise ambiguous ("my favorite nephew"), we don't know on the face of the will which of his two nephews Tate preferred. In this instance, virtually all courts permit extrinsic evidence to prove the identity of the intended beneficiary. The will would probably be reformed to allow either Don or Zeke, as the case may be, to take one-half of Tate's estate.

Sally, of course, would receive the remaining one-half of Tate's estate.

Answer to Question 17

Do any of the documents, either alone or together, constitute a valid will?

These facts require that we scrutinize all of the documents both separately and together. We will call the document found in Tawny's top desk drawer the "primary document." Does this document constitute a valid testamentary instrument? Except for the fact that it does not contain a detailed dispository scheme, it does qualify as a holographic instrument. For a holographic will to be valid, its "material provisions" must be in the testator's handwriting, and the will must be signed by the testator. (UPC § 2-502(b)). The primary document satisfies both of these requirements.

But the primary document cannot stand alone. It needs other documents to flesh out Tawny's dispository scheme.

Let's consider Document #3 first. It seems relatively clear that this Document was intended by Tawny to serve as a codicil to the primary document. It is labelled "Page 2" and was probably intended by Tawny to be attached to and read as a part of the primary document. Document #3 satisfies the requirements for a holographic will--it is entirely in Tawny's handwriting and it is signed by her.

But the primary document and Document #3 together do not constitute an entire dispository scheme by themselves. The primary document refers to other documents and Document #3 refers to "everything else." It's clear that we need other documents to complete Tawny's scheme. The other documents are Documents #1 and #2. We are able to include these documents under the doctrine of *incorporation by reference*. Under this doctrine, a writing that is already in existence when a will is executed may be incorporated into the will by reference, if the language of the will manifests this intent and describes the writing sufficiently to permit its identification. See UPC § 2-510. Under the incorporation-by-reference doctrine, elements that don't independently satisfy testamentary formalities (*e.g.*, witnesses, or the testator's signature) may become part of a will.

For incorporation by reference to apply, there must be a basic or primary document into which the other pre-existing documents can be incorporated. This primary document must, of course, satisfy testamentary formalities.

Sam, who will prefer that Tawny be deemed to have died intestate, will contend that if the primary document (and, in this case, the codicil to the primary document) is a holographic instrument, then other documents may be incorporated into it by reference only if the other documents also satisfy the requirements for holographic instruments. Thus, he would argue, the "material provisions" of the other documents, not just those contained in the primary document, must be in the testator's handwriting. Because Documents #1 and #2 are not entirely in Tawny's handwriting, there is no integrated holographic will and the whole testamentary scheme dies.

The proponents of the will will reply that as long as the primary document and the codicil are entirely in the testatrix's handwriting and signed by her, the "material provisions" requirement for a valid holographic will is satisfied. Because this approach would probably satisfy Tawny's dispository scheme better, it is likely to prevail here. The proponents may be able to show that the blanks in Document #1, the preprinted deed, were completed by Tawny in her own handwriting. If they were, the proponents could reasonably argue that the holographic requirements were satisfied as to Document #1 as well. As for Document #2, the proponents could argue that the handwritten amendment from "brother Bob" to "son Sam" also created a holographic instrument.

Sam will next contend that the incorporation-by reference-doctrine should *not* be applied for two reasons. First, the writings sought to be incorporated (Documents #1 and #2) may not have been in existence when the primary document incorporating them was written--a condition for incorporating them. (*See,* UPC § 2-510.) There is no direct proof in the facts that Documents #1 and #2 pre-dated the primary document. However, a jury could reasonably infer that both writings were already in existence. Why else did Tawny refer specifically to *two* pieces of paper that disposed of her property?

Second, Sam will point out that although the primary document refers to "two pieces of paper," there are actually three documents (four, if one counts the note clipped to the deed as a separate document), and that the primary document should therefore be discounted as unreliable and ambiguous. But this argument is not persuasive. Because Document #3 is a holographic codicil and the note clipped to the deed really superfluous, we are left with only two documents-- Documents #1 and #2.

In summary, there is probably sufficient evidence for a factfinder to conclude that the primary document is a valid holographic will which incorporates Documents #1 and #2 by reference, and that Document #3 is a valid holographic codicil to that will.

Is Document #1 (the deed) by itself a testamentary document?

In the event that the factfinder refuses to apply the incorporation-by-reference doctrine to incorporate Documents #1 and #2 within the primary document and its codicil (Document #3), Ann could probably still successfully claim that Document #1 constituted a valid will because it was incorporated into the holographic note attached by the paper clip, and the note attached incorporated the deed by reference through the use of the words "*this* is "and "enjoys *it*."

Assuming all the documents are read together as one integrated will, how should Tawny's estate be distributed?

The cash (the "money"): Shirley and Ann might contend that Tawny's cash should be part of the residuary clause ("everything else") because (1) the gift to Bob was cancelled; and (2) the attempted bequest to Sam was not accompanied by the necessary testamentary formalities (*i.e.*, it is not itself a valid holographic codicil because it was not signed). However, it may very well be the case that Tawny realized when she read the typewritten note that she had mistakenly typed Bob's name instead of Sam's and really meant Sam all along.

There is a second theory on which the attempted replacement bequest to Sam can be upheld: UPC § 2-503 validates a document or writing that doesn't meet testamentary formalities "if the proponent of the document or writing establishes by clear and convincing evidence that the decedent intended the . . . writing to constitute . . . (iii) an addition to or an alteration of the will. . . ." The Comment to this section makes it clear that it's designed to cover the situation in which a testator crosses out some text and substitutes new text, without a new signature and a new set of witnesses. The change from Bob to Sam probably satisfies this test, though there is no "clear and convincing" evidence that the change was made by Tawny herself rather than by someone else (say, Sam).

It's probable that one of these arguments for validating the substitution of Sam for Bob will be accepted by the court, and that the money will pass to Sam.

The ABC stock: Under the UPC, the beneficiary of a devise of stock is entitled to additional securities of the same organization owned by the testator at death by reason of action initiated by that organization (UPC § 2-605(a)(1)). Therefore, Shirley would receive all of the ABC stock.

Jewelry: Bob and Shirley could argue that the jewelry box should not go to Ann as jewelry but should fall instead into the residuary clause (*i.e.*, it is personal property which has not otherwise been disposed of by Tawny's other testamentary documents). Assuming, however, that Tawny (1) possessed the jewelry box on June 1, 1998 (when the will may first have been written), and (2) has not acquired or disposed of any other items which could be characterized as jewelry since that date, the term "jewelry" probably meant the jewelry box. Oral testimony would be accepted on these points. Ann should probably receive the jewelry box.

Furniture: Ann might argue that the devise of the house included the furniture within it. (How else could she enjoy the dwelling as much as Tawny?) But furniture in a home is usually considered personal property of the testatrix and is not usually deemed part of the realty. There's no easy answer here, but because there is no clear indication that Tawny intended the furniture to go to Ann, it would probably be included in the residuary estate.

Summary:

Assuming the integrated will (the primary document, Document #1 and its attached note, Document #2, and the codicil in Documents #3) comprises Tawny's testamentary scheme: Ann should receive the house, the jewelry box, and one-third of the furniture; Sam should receive the $100,000 in cash; Bob should receive one-third of the furniture; and Shirley should receive all of the ABC stock and one-third of the furniture.

It should be mentioned that if the entire set of documents is *not* admitted to probate as a single integrated will, Tawny's testamentary scheme will probably be reduced only to the disposition of the real estate to Ann under Document #1. All else would fail and Sam and Ann would divide equally between them all the rest of Tawny's property.

Answer to Question 18

1. Who is entitled to the trust estate and in what amounts?

Every trust must have a trust res, a trustee, and named or ascertainable beneficiaries. The first two requirements are clearly satisfied by these facts (the assets of Silver's estate constitute the trust res and Thompson is the trustee). The beneficiaries are not named, but can they be ascertained? The answer is "yes." The "employees of the bar and grill" at the time of Silver's death can be ascertained by a review of the payroll records. Thompson had no discretion which employees to designate; any one of them (Able, Baker or Charley) could enforce the trust.

Silver's heirs will contend, however, that the trust fails because Thompson never designated the amount which each employee would receive. They will argue that a resulting trust would arise in their favor.

In a situation such as this, courts will normally attempt to determine whether the trustee had any real discretion to depart from the testator's mandate in designating the beneficiaries. (Parol evidence is ordinarily admissible upon this point.) In most cases, the courts will decide that the testator did not intend to give the trustee this latitude.

Here, the amount to be allocated to each of the employees was, presumably, to be based upon some verifiable measure (*e.g.*, years worked, position held, dedication, attendance, work attitudes, etc.). If Thompson's successor trustee were unable to determine how the trust assets should be distributed, the court would probably determine that the three employees should share equally. Silver obviously wanted to distribute his estate among his employees. Presumably, he would have preferred an equal distribution among them to distribution to his next of kin in intestacy.

2. What standards determine whether Thompson has breached the duty of trust?

The actions of a trustee are ordinarily judged by the "reasonably prudent investor" standard. Under this doctrine, a trustee must ordinarily act with the same care and prudence toward the trust assets as he would with respect to his own funds.

In some jurisdictions, a trustee may make only certain types of investments (government bonds, blue chip stocks, etc.). However, we'll assume that this jurisdiction does not follow this rule and that Thompson was free to operate the bar and to own the stock of Red Company and Blue Company.

Thompson's estate might claim that he was given greater latitude than most trustees in investing assets of the trust, because he was specifically authorized to utilize his "discretion." While it is possible for a trustor to enlarge a trustee's authority to make investments beyond the "reasonably prudent investor" standard, the trustor must express this intent clearly. It is unlikely the word "discretion," without more, would be construed to expand the usual "reasonably prudent investor" standard. Instead, the court will probably conclude that Thompson's discretion was to be exercised in accordance with the "reasonably prudent investor" standard.

Did Thompson breach the "reasonably prudent investor" rule by retaining the bar and grill?

The next of kin will argue that a bar and grill is an inherently speculative investment, even in the hands of a sound operator, and is thus never suitable property for a trust. They will argue that the bar should have been sold immediately. However, modern courts have expanded the notion of what constitutes a suitable trust investment, and are willing to let the possibility of unusually high profits offset unusual risk. Given that the bar was originally part of the trust property, and that it was operating profitably at the beginning, the court would probably not hold that it was a breach of trust for Thompson to try to operate the bar initially.

A better argument is that Thompson should not have retained the bar and grill for a second year (during which time the business lost $15,000). The beneficiaries could argue that the success of this type of establishment requires personalized skill and experience which Thompson may not have possessed. (The facts fail to indicate whether Thompson had any prior background in running a bar and grill.) Thompson's estate will assert in rebuttal, however, that he had successfully operated the bar and grill during the initial year (as evidenced by the $10,000 profit during this period), and that there was no reason to suspect that he would not do at least as well in the second year.

Additional facts are needed to determine whether Thompson's estate will be liable. If, for example, Silver had regularly achieved a $50,000 per year profit prior to his death, there would be a persuasive argument that Thompson should have concluded after his first year of operation of the business that he lacked the skill to run it effectively. On the other hand, if Thompson's estate can show that he did as well as Silver or can identify independent and unforeseeable market factors which reduced the restaurant's profits, the estate should be able to escape liability.

Thompson's estate will also contend that Silver's will implicitly authorized retention of the bar and grill for two years (it was not until the conclusion of that period that the principal and accrued interest were to be distributed). This argument would probably fail. The court would probably determine that Silver's instructions were (1) not intended to override the "reasonably prudent investor" rule, and (2) merely prescribed an outside date by which the establishment was to be sold.

If it is determined that Thompson breached the "reasonably prudent investor" standard, his estate would be liable for all losses which should have been avoided. That is, the estate would be liable for: (1) the difference between the fair market value of the business at the time it should have been sold, and the amount received at the actual sale; (2) the operating losses incurred after the time the business should have been sold; and (3) interest on items (1) and (2) above.

Thompson's estate will argue that any losses computed under this formula should be reduced by the profits ($10,000) earned during Thompson's first year of operations. If the property should have been sold by Thompson promptly, or soon after the *first* year began— so that retaining the business at all was a single breach of trust — this argument might succeed, because gains and losses from a single breach of trust may be offset against each other, according to most courts. If, on the other hand, it was reasonable (and not a breach of trust) for Thompson to keep the business during the first year, and the breach of trust arose only after it started to lose money during the second year, then Thompson's estate would probably *not* be entitled to an offset of profits against losses — a trustee may not offset losses from a breach of trust by using profits made from other, reasonable trust investments.

Did Thompson's election to accept Blue Company stock in lieu of the fair market value of Red Company shares violate the "reasonably prudent investor" rule?

The trust beneficiaries will contend that it was imprudent for Thompson to invest in a new, highly speculative business (experimental electronics). Thompson's estate could respond by pointing out (correctly) that the trust deferred any capital gains tax on the Red shares by accepting the stock-swap, whereas it would have had to pay these taxes if it had sold the Red Company stock. Tax considerations certainly are taken into account in determining whether a trustee has behaved "prudently." However, the risks from a new speculative electronics investment were so great that the court would probably conclude that these far outweighed the benefits from tax deferral, and that a "reasonably prudent investor" would have opted for the sale of Red Company stock instead of the stock swap. Thompson's estate will be liable for the sum of $4,500 (the difference between the fair market value of the Red Company stock and the sale price of the Blue Company stock) less the net capital gains resulting from both transactions, plus interest upon the net after taxes, commencing from the date when the Red Company stock could have been sold for $75 per share.

Did Thompson's failure to sell the bar, and to take the Blue stock, constitute a failure to diversify?

In recent years, courts have begun to hold that an investment strategy is "reasonably prudent" only if it is reasonably *diversified. See*, e.g., Rest. 3d of Trusts, § 227(b). ("In making and implementing investment decisions, the trustee has a duty to diversify the investments of the trust unless, under the circumstances, it is prudent not to do so.") A trust corpus consisting only of two investments, one of which is completely illiquid (the bar), is almost certainly insufficiently diversified. The fact that these were the sole investments left by Silver to the trust does not matter — the trustee has a duty to sell pre-existing trust assets where necessary to achieve diversification, unless the trust instrument explicitly provides otherwise. Therefore, the court will probably hold that Thompson had the obligation to sell part of the Red stock (or part of the Blue stock once he received it in the swap), and perhaps to sell the bar, solely on diversification grounds. If so, the measure of damages would be the difference between the performance of a reasonably diversified portfolio and the actual performance achieved by Thompson here.

Answer to Question 19

1. Was the typewritten document dated September 17, 1985 a valid will?

The answer is no. The document does not satisfy the formal requirements for a valid will. It was not signed by the testator. It was not acknowledged as a testamentary document before two witnesses. The testator's signature was not witnessed by at least two subscribing witnesses.

2. Did the June 15, 1986 document create a valid holographic will?

The beneficiaries can make a very plausible argument that the June 15, 1986 document created a valid holographic will.

Hoby will contend that the June 15, 1986 document is *not* a valid holographic will because (1) it is not signed, but merely initialed; (2) it does not specifically incorporate by reference the distribution scheme set forth in the September 27, 1985 writing (and so contains no disposition of Tait's estate); (3) a subsequent document may not incorporate a prior document which is itself invalid as a testamentary document; and (4) even if the September 27, 1985 document were incorporated, there would still be no valid holographic will because the "material provisions" (*i.e.*, those describing the disposition of Tait's estate) are typewritten.

But the beneficiaries will reply as follows. First, the initials of the testator are ordinarily viewed as sufficient to satisfy the signature requirement in a will. Second, the word "adopt" should be construed to mean "incorporate by reference," because Tait obviously intended to give effect to the testamentary scheme in the September 27, 1985 writing. (It would not be helpful for the beneficiaries to argue that the word "adopt" should be read as "republish;" the majority view is that an invalid will *cannot* be republished.) Finally, the requirement that "material provisions" must be in the testator's handwriting is arguably satisfied by the words "I adopt" (*i.e.*, "I incorporate by reference") the typewritten draft. There is every reason to interpret the two documents together in this manner because they give effect to Tait's testamentary intentions instead of leaving her intestate.

The beneficiaries should prevail. Therefore, the will (comprised of the September 27, 1985 and June 15, 1986 documents together) is valid.

3. Assuming Tait had a valid will, how should her estate be distributed?

Minco stock: Although Sal predeceased Tait, his daughter (Helen) would step into Sal's position under the antilapse provisions. (UPC § 2-603(b)). Helen, although adopted, would be treated as Sal's issue (UPC §§ 1-201(5), 2-114(b)).

Under the UPC, the beneficiary of a devise of stock is entitled to additional securities of the same organization owned by the testator at death by reason of action initiated by that organization. (UPC § 2-605(a)). The question does not indicate that the additional Minco stock was acquired in some other way. Therefore, Helen would receive all 300 shares of Minco stock unless Hoby was able to show that the additional shares of Minco stock were actually purchased by Tait from her general funds.

Zebco stock: Hoby will contend that the gift of Oilco stock has been extinguished by ademption, and that, therefore, he is entitled to the Zebco stock via the residuary clause. However, the beneficiary of a gift of stock in one organization is entitled to the securities of another organization acquired by the testator as a result of a merger between the two companies. (UPC § 2-605(a)(2)). Therefore, Diane is entitled to the shares of Zebco stock.

Abco stock: Bill will contend that the Abco stock passes to him because it was found in the wall safe. But Hoby will argue -- probably successfully -- that stock is ordinarily not viewed as a "personal effect." The Abco stock should pass to Hoby under the residuary clause.

Jewelry: Tait's personal jewelry will be considered a part of her "personal effects." Because it was found in the wall safe, Bill will argue that the jewelry passes to him. Hoby will assert that because she put her jewelry into the safe only after the will was made, Tait did not intend a specific testamentary act; in any event, the act did not comply with any of the necessary testamentary formalities. Thus, Hoby would contend, the gift to Bill should fail.

However, under the *events of independent significance* doctrine, a will may dispose of property as a consequence of acts or events which have significance apart from their testamentary effect. (UPC § 2-512). Since placing items in a safe has a purpose which is non-testamentary in nature (*e.g.*, the testator may intend simply to prevent the articles from being misplaced or stolen), the fact that Tait's act also had a testamentary effect (effectuating the gift to Bill) would be irrelevant. Thus, Tait's jewelry should pass to Bill.

Bank account: The bank account would pass to Hoby under the residuary clause of Tait's will.

4. If the will is not valid, how would Tait's estate be distributed?

Under intestacy principles, Hoby would receive the entire estate. The reasoning: all of Tait's surviving descendants are also Hoby's descendants and Hoby does not have other surviving descendants who are not descendants of Tait. (UPC § 2-102(1)(ii)).

5. Result if Hoby had predeceased Tait, and the latter had then married John:

Hoby's interest would lapse, since he would not be considered a surviving spouse. John would be considered a pretermitted spouse and would take an intestate share (UPC § 2-301). However, John would not get an intestate share of the whole estate — any devises to a child of the testator's prior marriage (or to a descendant of that child, under § 2-603's antilapse provision) would first be carved out, and John would then get his intestate share of the balance. Thus the Minco stock (which goes to Sal's daughter Helen), and the Zebco stock (which goes to Tait's daughter Diane) would be removed from the computation; John would then get the first $100,000 plus one-half of the balance of the estate. (UPC § 2-102(4)).

Other gifts would have to be abated to satisfy John's intestate share. The order in which items are abated is set forth in UPC § 3-902: first, property not disposed of by will; then, residuary devises; then, general devises; finally, specific devises. Assuming there is no property passing to John outside of the will (the facts don't point to any), residuary devises, which include the Abco stock and the bank accounts (worth a total of $105,000), would be abated first. There are no general devises. The jewelry (the only asset not yet taken into account) is a specific devise; John would take half the value of this jewelry after the first $5,000 in jewelry value.

Answer to Question 20

Was the September 20, 1995 document a valid will?

The September 20, 1995 document does not satisfy the UPC's requirements for a valid will. It's not signed, and it's not acknowledged by two witnesses. *See,* UPC § 2-502(a). However, the document may qualify for probate as a holographic will. To be valid as a holographic will, a document need not be witnessed, but it must be signed by the testator, and "material portions" of it must be in the testator's handwriting. UPC § 2-502(b).

Among the beneficiaries, Bessie is the one who would gain the most if Timothy is deemed to have died intestate. She will argue that the September 20, 1995 document was not a valid holographic will because (1) it was not signed by Timothy, and (2) it did not clearly and unambiguously dispose of Timothy's entire estate. The document refers to "one-half" of something, but it's not clear what that "something" is. Did Timothy mean one-half of the residue after subtracting the stock in the notebook he was keeping (although the facts don't tell us when he started to keep the notebook)? Or did he mean one-half of the entire estate? Or one-half of his stock only? We don't really know, and that strengthen's Bessie's argument that the document should not be accepted because it does not contain a clear dispository scheme.

On the other hand, The Boys Club will assert: (1) by writing his own name in the body of the document, Timothy satisfied the signature requirement (UPC § 2-502(b) does not say that the testator's signature must be at the foot of the document), and (2) a reasonable interpretation of the document is that Timothy wanted to divide his estate evenly between Bessie and The Boys Club because Timothy preceded the words "one-half" with the words "I...make this will." Given the usual desire of probate courts to effectuate the testator's wishes by accepting documents which display a testamentary intent, the September 20, 1995 document will probably be received as a valid holographic will.

If the September 20, 1995 document was not itself a valid will, was it republished, or otherwise made valid, by the June 30, 1998 document?

If the court does not accept the September 20, 1995 document as a valid holographic will, The Boys Club will make the following alternative arguments:

The June 30, 1998 document appears to be a valid holographic codicil to the September 20, 1995 document. First of all, it refers to "my previous will." Also, it purports to dispose of Timothy's property; it's in Timothy's handwriting; and it's signed by Timothy. Relying on these facts, The Boys Club will argue first that the June 30, 1998 codicil *republished* the September 20, 1995 writing. Republication can occur under the following circumstances: T executes valid will #1. Later, he executes will #2, expressly revoking will #1. Still later, T destroys will #2 by physical act. Finally, T executes a document which recites that it is a codicil to will #1. Will #1 is revived, provided it is still in existence. Republication is recognized by statute in many states. However, in most jurisdictions, a document which is not itself valid as a will *cannot* be revived by publication.

More persuasively, The Boys Club will contend that the June 30, 1998 document was itself a complete and valid holographic will (rather than a codicil to an existing will) that incorporated the September 20, 1995 document by reason of the reference to "my former will." Although Timothy's language does not specifically incorporate the prior document, this argument will probably succeed. Because Timothy obviously believed that the first document was valid (as evidenced by his reference to his "previous will"), this result would effectuate his testamentary intent.

Finally, The Boys Club (as well as Dorothy) will argue that the two documents (September 20, 1995 and June 30, 1998) should be read together as a single will, enforceable under UPC § 2-503's provision validating certain documents that don't meet all the testamentary formalities. Under that provision, non-compliance with the formalities is ignored "if the proponent of the document or writing establishes by clear and convincing evidence that the decedent intended the document or writing to constitute (i) the decedent's will [or] (iii) an addition to or an alteration of the will. . . ." The September 20, 1995 document probably qualifies under (i) of this test, and the June 30, 1998 document probably qualifies under (iii).

Summary:

The court will probably accept the argument that the two documents should be read together to form one integrated testamentary document disposing of Timothy's entire estate.

Does the black book become part of the testamentary scheme?

Because the black book does not on its face meet any of the testamentary formalities, it cannot by itself constitute either a will or a codicil. However, under the doctrine of incorporation by reference, a writing in existence when a will is executed may be incorporated into the will if the will's language manifests this intent and the will describes the writing sufficiently to identify it. Because (1) the June 30, 1998 document clearly refers to "stocks listed in my black book;" (2) the black book was found in the same safe deposit box as the 1998 document and contained a handwritten list of stock transactions; and (3) the black book existed on June 30, 1998, the requirements for incorporation-by-reference are met. Therefore, the black book becomes part of the testamentary scheme because the June 30, 1998 document is part of that scheme. (As to the effect of changes to the black book made after June 30, 1998, *see* the subsequent discussion.)

What is the effect of the June 30, 1998 document upon Timothy's testamentary scheme?

If we conclude that the June 30, 1998 document is an integral part of Timothy's testamentary scheme, we need to determine just what the effect of that document is.

It's unclear from the June 30, 1998 document ("Bessie doesn't need all that") whether Timothy wanted to *revoke* the portion devised to Bessie in the Sept. 20, 1995 document, or intended instead to *reduce* Bessie's one-half share of the entire estate by the value of the stocks listed in the black book. As we shall see, however, this ambiguity does not have to be resolved — whether construed as a revocation or as a reduction, Bessie will still get the same amount--$30,000.

If the June 30, 1998 document is interpreted as a mere reduction of Bessie's interest, Bessie will get half the estate ($70,000), less the value of the stocks ($40,000), or $30,000. If the document is interpreted as a revocation of Bessie's portion, then the distribution will be as follows: (1) The Boys Club will receive one-half of Timothy's estate ($70,000); (2) Bessie's child, Dorothy, will receive the stocks (value--$40,000); and (3) the remainder of Timothy's estate will pass as in *intestacy* (because there is no residuary clause). Bessie, as Timothy's sister, would then be entitled to receive all of the assets which were not specifically disposed of ($30,000). (UPC § 2-103(3)). Because Dorothy claims through Bessie, who is still alive, she would get nothing in intestacy.

Dorothy's interest in the stocks will not fail even though Dorothy was not specifically named in the June 30, 1998 document. Extrinsic evidence will be admissible to prove that she was Bessie's only daughter.

What is the effect of the stock transactions which occurred after June 30, 1998?

Bessie will wish to contend that entries in the black notebook made after June 30, 1998 (the date of the second document) should be disallowed. She will argue that Timothy's act in making these entries should not be given testamentary effect because they did not comply with any of the necessary testamentary formalities. Accordingly, the XYZ stock should be part of the intestate estate.

Dorothy will assert that the XYZ stock is hers by virtue of the doctrine of *"events of independent significance" ("EIS")*. Under this theory, a will may dispose of property by reference to acts or events which have a significance apart from their testamentary effect. (UPC § 2-512). Dorothy will argue Timothy's act in inserting the purchase of XYZ stock into the black book had independent significance to him (*i.e.*, it assisted him in recording and recalling his stock transactions to permit him to make sale-and-purchase decisions).

Bessie will reply to this argument by contending that when the "event" which is alleged to be of independent significance is a writing, the EIS doctrine should not apply. Instead, especially on these facts, the writing should be controlled by the "incorporation by reference" doctrine. Because the "incorporation by reference" doctrine requires that the writing be in existence at the time the will is executed, and the reference to XYZ stock was not in existence at that time (June 30, 1998), the XYZ stock would not fall within the transactions incorporated by the black book.

Although a close question, Dorothy's "events of independent significance" test will probably prevail and she will receive the XYZ stock. Does she also have a right to the $10,000 resulting from the sale of 100 shares of ABC stock? Probably not. The court is likely to conclude that the doctrine of ademption applies. (If the subject of a specific bequest is not in the testator's estate at death, it is said to be adeemed or extinguished.) Dorothy can argue that the sale of the ABC stock and the simultaneous purchase of the XYZ stock were a single transaction whose benefits all belong to her. But the court is likely to divide the estate into two separate ingredients, stock and cash. The ABC and XYZ stock will go to Dorothy and the cash will be divided between The Boys Club and Bessie as calculated in our Summary below.

Summary:

Based upon the foregoing discussion, it is likely that The Boys Club will receive $70,000 in cash, Bessie will receive $30,000 in cash, and Dorothy will receive the ABC and XYZ stock.

Answer to Question 21

1. Did Thor die testate or intestate?

Sandra (who would receive Thor's estate if Thor died intestate by virtue of being sole beneficiary under Ethel's will) will contend that (1) Will 1 was expressly cancelled by the note which was attached to it (*i.e.*, a will may be revoked by a subsequent document which was executed with the necessary testamentary formalities, and the attached note was made in accordance with the requirements of a valid holographic will); and (2) Will 2 is invalid, since it was (i) not in Thor's handwriting (preventing it from being construed as a valid holographic will), and (ii) attested by only one subscribing witness (preventing it from being considered a valid formal will). Sandra will assert that Thor died intestate.

The heirs under both wills (John, Gil and Warren) will make the following two arguments in favor of the court's finding either Will 1 or Will 2 valid (either one will protect their interests equally):

Doctrine of dependent relative revocation ("DDRR"): Under DDRR, when a will is revoked by a new (but invalid) will which is made simultaneously with the act of revocation, the first will is revived, provided the court determines that the testator would have probably desired this result. Because the differences between Will 1 and Will 2 are now moot (*i.e.*, there is no need to invade the trust corpus because Ethel has died), the heirs will contend that Will 1 should be reinstated under DDRR if Will 2 is deemed invalid.

Sandra will contend that: (1) in some states, DDRR will not be applied where the revocation was done expressly in a writing (*i.e.*, rather than by physical act), and (2) the revocatory act did not occur simultaneously with Will 2 (Will 1 was not expressly revoked until *one day after* T signed Will 2).

Assuming this jurisdiction applies DDRR even in the face of an express revocation, DDRR would probably be accepted here to revive Will 1. The one-day gap between the signing of Will 2 and the express revocation of Will 1 would probably be viewed as being sufficiently "simultaneous." This view would permit Thor's estate to pass by Will 1, rather than in intestacy. Thor's estate will probably be distributed pursuant to Will 1.

Incorporation by reference: Alternatively, the heirs will stake their argument on the doctrine of incorporation by reference. Under this doctrine, a writing which is in existence when a will is made may be incorporated by reference, if the language of the will manifests this intent and describes the writing sufficiently to permit its identification (UPC § 2-510). The heirs might argue: (1) the note that was attached to Will 1 was a valid holographic will because it was in the testator's handwriting and signed by her, and (2) the holographic will, by means of the statement "I have made another will," incorporated Will 2 into the terms of a valid holographic document.

Sandra will contend: (1) the validity of a holographic will should be judged by looking at the entire document, including the portions incorporated: here, the requirement that a holographic will contain "material portions" in the testator's handwriting is not met. On the contrary, Will 2, which contains all the material terms, was entirely typewritten. And (2) the language that is asserted to be the language of incorporation ("I have made another will") does not evidence a clear intent to incorporate Will 2; it is merely a statement of past action which does not specifically refer to Will 2.

On the issues, the heirs will probably win. The DDRR argument is likely to prevail. If it does not, there is at least a respectable chance that the incorporation-by-reference argument will prevail. The court is not likely to find that Thor died intestate under these circumstances.

2. *Assuming Thor died testate, how should her estate be distributed?*

If we assume that Thor died testate, we don't actually need to know whether the operative will is Will 1 or Will 2. Now that Ethel is dead, the two documents are functionally identical.

Was the $10,000 to Robert Rood an outright gift to him, or was it to be held in trust for Carrie?

Carrie will contend that because the $10,000 bequest to Robert Rood was "to be used" for her education, a trust for her benefit was created, and Robert has to spend the $10,000 as prescribed. Robert will argue -- successfully -- that no trust was created because the language used was not clear enough. When Thor intended to create a trust, she used language which was clear and unequivocal, as when she used the terms "trustee" and "trust" language in the second paragraph of both her wills. Thor's instructions with respect to Carrie will probably be construed as precatory in nature and Robert Rood should prevail on this issue.

Would Sandra be entitled to receive anything?

Sandra would receive nothing, since there was a specific "gift over" provision to Thor's heirs upon Ethel's death. Ethel's interest in the trust was only a life interest.

What shares would John, Gil and Warren receive?

When a will provides that a decedent's property is to be distributed to her "heirs," distribution is usually made according to intestacy principles. Where there is no surviving parent and no descendants of the testator, distribution is made to the descendants of the decedent's parents, by representation (UPC § 2-103(3)). The distribution is made "per capita at each generation," the division of the estate starting at the highest level in which there are living members (UPC § 2-106). The highest level at which there are living members is that shared by John and Gil and by Warren's deceased parent, the child of Thor's deceased sister Bessie. Therefore, the estate is split into thirds. John and Gil take one-third each. Warren takes his parent's one-third by representation. Thus, John, Gil and Warren would each receive one-third of Thor's remaining estate (after the $10,000 gift to Rood).

3. *Assuming Thor died intestate, how should her estate be distributed?*

Under the UPC, when there is no spouse, the decedent's descendants take by right of representation. § 2-103(1). Because Ethel was Thor's only descendant and she was alive at the time of Thor's death (intestacy rights are fixed at the testator's death), Sandra, as the beneficiary under Ethel's will, would be entitled to Thor's entire estate.

Answer to Question 22

Was Will #1 valid?

A will is valid even though it was witnessed by an interested person (UPC § 2-505(b)). Since Will #1 was witnessed by two persons, it appears to be valid.

Was Will #1 revoked by Will #2?

Where a testator executes a second will which is inconsistent with his earlier wills and codicils, the earlier wills are canceled. Thus Mary and John would argue that, since the testamentary scheme of Will #2 is irreconcilable with Will #1, Will #1 was invalidated.

However, Allen would argue that Will #2 was induced by John's fraud. Fraud in the inducement occurs where the testator understands the provisions of the will he is signing, but has been induced to make provisions that he would not have made had he not been deceived as to underlying facts. Here, Allen can make a strong claim that John's false statements about Allen's criminal activities constituted fraud in the inducement, leading Tom to remove Allen from the revised will.

Courts sometimes deny probate to a will that is the product of fraud in the inducement. However, where only some clauses, rather than the whole will, are induced by fraud, the court usually accepts the will for probate and uses the doctrine of constructive trust (discussed below) to remedy the fraud. Since there is no sign that the entire Will #2 was the product of fraud (*e.g.*, there's no evidence that the removal of the reference to David was accomplished by fraud), the court will probably admit Will #2, and regard Will #1 as having been revoked by Tom's adoption of Will #2.

Was Will #1 cancelled?

Even if Will #2 is found to be completely invalid for fraud, the court might find that Will #1 was cancelled. Drawing lines through a will with the intention of canceling it will revoke that document. Tom arguably canceled Will #1 by drawing lines through it. Thus, even if Will #2 is completely invalid due to John's fraud, Will #1 has still been negated.

However, the doctrine of dependent relative revocation ("DDRR") may be applicable. Under this theory, if one revokes a will under the *mistaken belief* that a simultaneous, alternative will is effective, the earlier will may be reinstated (provided the court believes that this is the result the testator would have wanted).

If Will #1 was revoked upon the belief that Will #2 was valid, but Will #2 was in fact invalid because of John's fraud, Will #1 should arguably be reinstated. However, there is no proof that Will #2 was made simultaneously with the cancellation of Will #1. Nevertheless, the fact that Will #1 was in the same safe deposit box as Will #2 permits an inference that the latter was created concurrently with the cancellation of the first. This result would probably be what Tom would have desired. Thus, Will #1 could possibly be revived.

Disposition under Will #1:

If Will #1 is valid, Mary would receive $80,000 ($50,000, plus 1/4 of the $120,000 residue), John, $45,000 ($15,000, plus 1/4 of the residue) and Allen, $45,000 (same computation as John). David had predeceased the making of Will #1, and therefore was arguably *not* within the class of "nephews and nieces" to which the residuary portion was to be distributed. However, UPC § 2-603(b)(2) permits the descendants of a deceased person who is included in a class description to take under the anti-lapse provision even though the deceased ancestor was dead at the time the will was executed. Thus, David's two children would step up into his share (1/4 of the $120,000 residue) under the anti-lapse statute and would receive $15,000 each.

Disposition under Will #2:

If Will #2 is found to be the valid will, the court will need to deal with the fact that John apparently committed fraud and thereby deprived Allen of the share he would have received absent the fraud. The rest of this discussion assumes that the court has concluded that such fraud did in fact occur.

Where a provision of a will is procured by fraud in the inducement, the court will generally attempt to redress the fraud by use of the doctrine of ***constructive trust***. That is, the court will leave the legal title to property as the will places it, but will require that the legal holder hold the property in trust for the benefit of the person who would have received it had the fraud not occurred. Usually the court also orders that the legal holder then convey legal title to the beneficiary of the constructive trust.

The court here will have to decide what Tom would have done had the fraud not taken place. The "conservative" approach is to assume that the fraud did not affect Mary's share, only the split between John and Allen. If the court makes this assumption, Mary will get $110,000 (the $50,000 specific bequest plus the same one-half of the $120,000 residue that the will by its terms gives her), and a constructive trust will be used to make Allen and John split the money ($90,000) that the will gives to John alone. That is, the court will declare $45,000 of John's proceeds subject to a constructive trust for the benefit of Allen, and would then compel John to convey this amount to Allen.

Alternatively, the court might conclude that absent the fraud, Tom would have decided to split the $30,000 specific bequest between John and Allen (so far, this is still the same as the "conservative" approach discussed above), but that the residuary would have been split equally among Mary, John and Allen. This approach has the merit of being similar to the pre-fraud approach taken by Tom. If the court did this, then Mary would take $90,000 (the $50,000 specific bequest plus 1/3 of the $120,000 residue), and John and Allen would split $110,000 (the $30,000 specific bequest to John plus 2/3's of the $120,000 residue). This approach, of course, penalizes the "innocent" Mary, but there is good authority and logic for it: Mary's innocence should not lead to her getting something that she would not have gotten absent John's fraud.

Disposition if Tom died intestate:

If Will #1 and Will #2 are both invalid (Will #1 because it was cancelled and Will #2 because it was the product of fraud), Tom's brothers and sisters (and the issue thereof by right of representation) would share his estate. The distribution is made "per capita at each generation," the division of the estate starting at the highest level in which there are living members (UPC § 2-106). The $200,000 would be divided into four parts (for Mary, Tom, Allen and David). Thus, Mary, Tom and Allen would each receive $50,000, and David's children would share the remaining $50,000.

Answer to Question 23

1. Disposition of Betty's estate:

We will assume that Betty's will was executed with the requisite testamentary formalities (the facts are silent as to this point).

Effect of simultaneous death:

Under UPC § 2-702, a beneficiary is not deemed to have "survived" the testator unless the beneficiary lives at least 120 hours following the testator's death. Therefore, for purposes of Betty's will, Wilma did not "survive" Betty. Consequently, the $100,000 goes to "the natural persons who are beneficiaries of Wilma's last will and testament. . . ."

While Wilma's final will probably excluded Bill (discussed below), Bill could point out that he was one of the three beneficiaries of Wilma's will *as that will was constituted when Betty's will was made* in 1990. Thus, Bill would claim that he is entitled to one-half of the $100,000 gift made by Betty.

Mary would argue, however, that the language in Betty's will should be read literally. Thus, Wilma's "*last* will and testament" (*i.e.*, the will as it stood at Wilma's death) designated only Mary as a "natural person" beneficiary.

Additionally, where there is an ambiguity in a will, the vague provision will ordinarily be construed in a manner which would effectuate the testator's probable intent. The term "last will and testament" could mean Wilma's will as it existed (1) in 1990 (when Betty's will was made), or (2) when Wilma died. However, Betty obviously wanted to bestow an additional gift upon those particular persons who were the objects of Wilma's bounty. Since Wilma finally decided to reward only Mary, not Bill, Betty would presumably have preferred to do the same.

State University is not a natural person, and therefore would not share in the gift.

In summary, Mary would receive the $100,000 bequest.

How should the balance of Betty's estate be distributed?

The balance of Betty's estate is left "to my children, share and share alike." Since both "children" predeceased Betty, the issues are (i) does the gift fail completely? and, (ii) if not, is it divided per capita, or per stirpes, among Betty's grandchildren?

Does the gift fail?

The gift does not fail — it is saved by the *antilapse* provision, UPC § 2-603(b). Assuming that the gift was a "class gift" (with the class being Betty's children), the operative language is § 2-603(b)(2): "[A] substitute gift is created in the surviving descendants of any deceased devisee." (The antilapse statute also applies, though slightly differently as discussed below, if the gift is found to be a non-class gift to each of Betty's children individually.)

How is the substitute gift divided? There are two different ways the balance of Betty's estate could be divided: (1) as a pure per stirpes gift, *i.e.*, a gift by representation, divided from the "root" of each of Betty's children, in which case Alice would get half, and George and Fred would split the other half; or (2) as a "per capita" gift, whereby Alice, George and Fred would share equally, since all have the same degree of consanguinity to Betty.

Alternative (1) will probably prevail here. Whether the gift to "my children" is considered a class gift or two individual gifts, the result under the UPC is the same. If the gift is a non-class (individual) gift to each of Betty's children, UPC § 2-603(b)(1) would make each of the two children a "deceased devisee"; that deceased devisee's descendants would then "take *by representation* the property to which the devisee would have been entitled had the devisee survived the testator." So Charles' share ($200,000) would be evenly split between his two descendants, George and Fred, and Jane's share (also $200,000) would pass to her sole descendant, Alice.

If the gift to "my children" is considered a class gift, the operative language is UPC § 2-603(b)(2), under which "Each deceased devisee's surviving descendants who are substituted for the deceased devisee take *by representation* the share to which the deceased devisee would have been entitled had the deceased devisee survived the testator." So here, too, the split would be $200,000 to Alice and $100,000 each to George and Fred.

There is a small chance that a court might construe the language "share and share alike" in Betty's devise to her "children" to mean that in the event the children should predecease Betty (and the antilapse statute should come into play) Betty would have wanted the grandchildren to also "share and share alike." But since the UPC antilapse provision makes its own substitute gift according to its own well-defined rules, it's unlikely that the court will take into account Betty's wishes in this way. Therefore, the "by representation" approach will probably prevail.

2. Disposition of Wilma's estate:

We will assume that Wilma's will and codicil were executed with the requisite testamentary formalities (the facts are silent as to these points).

A factual mistake which induces a testator to make a particular disposition is ordinarily **not** a basis for invalidating a will. However, some states may deny probate of a will if (1) the mistake appears upon the face of the document, **and** (2) the alternative disposition which the testator would have desired is inferable from the will. Extrinsic evidence of errors is *not* admissible. Since the mistake here does not appear on the face of the will, the codicil deleting Bill because of his "ingratitude" is valid.

Was Wilma's gift to her children a class gift?

It is unclear whether Wilma's gift to her children was (1) a class gift, or (2) a gift to each of her children, individually. If it was an individual gift to each child, then the codicil would simply cancel the gift to Bill. Since there is no residuary clause in Wilma's will, the 1/4 of the estate that would have gone to Bill would then pass by intestacy. In that event, Bill would take 1/2 of the 1/4, or 1/8 of the estate. This "individual gifts" interpretation is at least weakly buttressed by the codicil's statement, "I delete the gift to my son, Bill" (as opposed to, say, "I modify the gift to my children to include only Mary. . . .")

If, however, "my children" was intended to set up a class gift (with the class being Wilma's children), Mary would take the entire one-half of the estate.

Unfortunately for Bill, the term "children" is ordinarily viewed as denoting a class gift (*i.e.*, Wilma did *not* state something like, to "Bill and Mary, my children"). This ordinary construction probably outweighs the small countervailing weight to be given to the "I delete the gift to my son Bill" language. Thus, Mary and State University will probably share Wilma's estate equally.

Answer to Question 24

1. *Was the trust effectively terminated by Ball during his lifetime?*

An *inter vivos* trust is ordinarily irrevocable, unless the settlor expressly reserves the power to revoke the trust. Ball, however, specifically reserved the power to revoke the trust in this instance.

Thus, the question becomes whether that power was effectively exercised? Although the trust provided that this power was to be exercised only by a writing which was (i) signed by Ball, and (ii) delivered to the trustee, Sam will argue that Ball's oral communication to the trustee was sufficient to accomplish a revocation. However, a power to revoke is ordinarily narrowly construed — it can be exercised only in strict accordance with its terms. See Rest. 2d of Trusts, § 330 and Comment j thereto. Probably, therefore, Ball's phone call was not effective to revoke the trust during his lifetime.

2. *Is the trustee obligated to pay Pearl past or future alimony out of the income and, to the extent necessary, the principal of the trust?*

A spendthrift trust is one in which, by statute or the terms of the trust, the beneficiary is unable to voluntarily or involuntarily transfer his interest in the trust. Spendthrift trusts are valid in almost all jurisdictions, and bar creditors of a beneficiary from reaching his interest in the trust to satisfy a claim. However, in many states (and under the Second Restatement of Trusts) an ex-spouse or child of a trust beneficiary can override the spendthrift clause for the purpose of securing support. See Rest. 2d of Trusts, § 157(a). In other states, there are statutes which protect the interest of beneficiaries in a spendthrift trust, but only to the extent necessary to secure their proper care, maintenance and support.

Therefore, the trustee would probably be obliged to pay Pearl for past and future alimony out of the trust's income. Since Sam has only an *income interest* in the trust, and since even those states allowing the beneficiary's children or ex-spouse to reach the trust limit the invasion to the beneficiary's interest, the trustee cannot be compelled to pay Pearl out of the principal.

3. *Do Sam and Pearl have the legal power to terminate the trust?*

The interests in the trust are an equitable life estate in Sam and a contingent remainder in Carol, subject to open for other children who may be born to Sam. The contingency is that Carol must survive Sam (*i.e.*, Carol's interest does not vest until Sam's death).

The majority rule is that beneficiaries may compel termination of a trust if (1) all of the beneficiaries are legally competent and join in the request to terminate, and (2) termination will not defeat a material purpose of the settlor in creating the trust. See Rest. 2d of Trusts, § 337.

The first problem is that all beneficiaries must not only consent but have legal capacity to consent. While Sam is competent, Carol is a minor and, therefore, "incompetent." A guardian *ad litem* might be appointed to represent Carol's interests. Neither Sam nor Pearl, however, can be appointed as guardian *ad litem*, since they have interests which are adverse to Carol (*i.e.*, to the extent Sam or Pearl receive income from the trust, the trust res which would ultimately be distributed to Carol is diminished). Assuming that a guardian other than Sam or Pearl was appointed, valid consent could be given by all three present beneficiaries.

The second, bigger problem is the requirement that *all* beneficiaries consent. The class of Sam's children is open until Sam dies. Thus, the interests of potential, unborn children cannot be determined or adequately represented at this time. Therefore, the "consent by all beneficiaries" requirement probably cannot be satisfied at this time, and the trustee probably cannot be compelled to terminate the trust.

There is a last, probably fatal, difficulty: termination of the trust would violate a material purpose of the settlor in creating the trust. The choice of a spendthrift trust by Ball evidences his intention to provide a lifetime income interest to Sam, free from Sam's improvidence. This purpose would be defeated if the trust was revoked. See Rest. 2d of Trusts, § 337, Comment l.

Answer to Question 25

Which, if any, of the documents found in Taylor's safedeposit box may be admitted to probate?

Since the typewritten document bears no signature and is not witnessed, it lacks the requisite testamentary formalities. Thus, this document, standing alone, is *not* a valid will and, therefore, may not be admitted to probate. The handwritten document, however, is signed and evidences a testamentary intent (*i.e.*, it states, "this is the way I want my property to go"). It would therefore arguably qualify as a holographic will.

The beneficiaries could then argue that the doctrine of *incorporation by reference* should be applied. Under this doctrine, a writing which is in existence when a will was made and which is incorporated by the will, becomes part of the will (even though the separate writing was not created with the requisite testamentary formalities). UPC § 2-510. Here, the typewritten document obviously preceded the handwritten one (since the latter makes reference to the former), and the handwritten one clearly refers to the typewritten one (by the language, "The attached is the way I want my property to go. . . .") Therefore, the typewritten document should be incorporated into the valid holographic writing.

In response to this argument, Doris (who would prefer that Taylor be found to have died intestate) could contend that the incorporation-by-reference doctrine should not be applied here, because to do so would nullify the requirements for a valid holographic will. To be valid as a holographic will, a document must be signed by the testator, and contain "material portions" in the testator's handwriting. UPC § 2-502(b). Doris would argue that since the bulk of the provisions of the two documents taken together are typewritten, and the only one in handwriting is the residuary clause, the "material portions in the testator's handwriting" requirement is not satisfied if incorporation by reference is used.

However, the residuary clause is certainly a material portion, and the clause incorporating the typewritten document is another material portion; UPC § 2-502(b) doesn't require that *all* material portions be in the testator's handwriting, merely that some do. This requirement is apparently satisfied. Thus the court will probably hold that the handwritten note was a valid holographic will that successfully incorporated the typewriting.

Alternatively, the two documents together could be validated under UPC § 2-503's "harmless error" provision, by which a document that is shown by "clear and convincing evidence" to have been intended by the decedent as his will can be admitted to probate even though it does not meet testamentary formalities.

In summary, the two documents found in Taylor's safe deposit box probably together constitute her will.

What is the effect of the destruction of the home on the gift to Aunt Marie?

The devise of the home to Aunt Marie is a "specific" devise. Under the Uniform Probate Code, a specific devisee has the right to "any proceeds *unpaid* at death on fire or casualty insurance" on the specific devise. (UPC § 2-606(a)(3)). This clause does not help Marie, because here the proceeds had already been paid to Taylor prior to her death.

Aunt Marie might be able to benefit from UPC § 2-606(a)(6), which provides that "unless the facts and circumstances indicate that ademption of the devise was intended by the testator or ademption of the devise is consistent with the testator's manifested plan of distribution, [the specific devisee has the right to] the value of the specifically devised property to the extent the specifically devised property is not in the testator's estate at death and its value or replacement is not covered by [other paragraphs of § 2-606(a).]" Since Taylor never conveyed the house to anyone else (which would have weakened Marie's case that Taylor wanted her to have the house's value), and since the house was "transformed" into insurance proceeds only very recently, through no voluntary act by Taylor, Marie will probably convince the court that under § 2-606(a)(6), ademption should not apply and she should get the insurance proceeds (plus any other money needed to make up the value of the house before destruction).

What is the effect of the stock split upon the gift to Al of XYZ stock?

Under the UPC, a beneficiary of securities is entitled to any accretion of that stock resulting from action initiated by the corporation. (UPC § 2-605(a)(1)). Thus, Al would receive all 400 shares of XYZ stock.

What is the effect of the bequest of 20 shares of IBM to Frank?

A gift of stock when no such shares are owned by the testator is usually held to be a general bequest. This is especially true where, as here, the form of the gift is "100 shares of XYZ" rather than "*my* 100 shares of XYZ." Where the gift is found to be a general one, the executor is normally required to use the estate's cash to buy the specified property and pay it to the beneficiary. Thus Taylor's executor must purchase 20 shares of IBM stock from the residuary portion of the estate, and give those shares to Frank.

What is the effect of Sarah's death prior to Taylor?

A gift to a beneficiary who predeceases the testator ordinarily lapses. However, under the UPC's anti-lapse statute, if the beneficiary is the testator's grandparent, or a lineal descendant of the testator's grandparent, who died leaving descendants, the descendants take in place of the beneficiary. UPC § 2-603(b)(1). Although Sarah was a lineal descendant of Taylor's grandparents, she has no issue. Thus, the gift to Sarah will lapse. Where the lapsed gift is a gift of the complete residuary, the property involved passes by intestate succession.

Who takes the property passing by intestate succession?

Under the UPC, where the decedent is not survived by a spouse, the intestate succession is to the deceased's descendants. In this case, that would be Doris, Taylor's daughter. See UPC § 2-103(1). The question is whether the language "to my daughter Doris — NOTHING" affects the intestate distribution.

At common law, a testator cannot use words in the will to prevent a person from taking her intestate share of property not covered by the will — the only way to disinherit someone is to bequeath all property to others under the will. But UPC § 2-101(b) changes this result: "A decedent by will may expressly exclude or limit the right of an individual or class to succeed to property of the decedent passing by intestate succession." The Comments to this provision make it clear that testamentary language stating that X gets nothing suffices, even if the language does not expressly mention intestacy. Thus the language "to my daughter Doris — NOTHING" is sufficient to disinherit Doris. Instead, the residuary will go by intestate succession to the next in line, Taylor's brother Ben. See UPC § 2-103(3).

Multiple-Choice Questions

1. Rosa died intestate. She was survived by her husband Bill and their children, Tim and Tammy. Her net estate available for distribution is separate property of $200,000. How should her estate be distributed?

   (A) $50,000 to Bill; $75,000 each to Tim and Tammy.
   (B) $125,000 to Bill; $37,500 each to Tim and Tammy.
   (C) $100,000 to Bill; $50,000 each to Tim and Tammy.
   (D) $200,000 to Bill.

2. On July 1, Jim Williams died intestate from injuries received in an automobile accident. His wife Wanda died the next day from injuries received in the same accident. Jim and Wanda were survived by one child, Bob, and two grandchildren who are the children of the deceased daughter of Jim and Wanda. Jim's net estate available for distribution is $200,000. How should Jim's estate be distributed?

   (A) $125,000 to Wanda's estate; $37,500 to Bob; and $18,750 each to the two grandchildren.
   (B) $125,000 to Wanda's estate; $25,000 each to Bob and the two grandchildren.
   (C) Nothing to Wanda's estate; $100,000 to Bob; $50,000 each to the two grandchildren.
   (D) Nothing to Wanda's estate; $66,666 each to Bob and the two grandchildren.

3. Leonard and Evelyn were married ten years ago. They had no issue. Five years ago, Leonard executed a will leaving everything to Evelyn, if she survived him; if she failed to survive him, the estate was to go to Leonard's mother and father in equal shares. Leonard's sister Sue and his brother-in-law Ken witnessed this will. Last year, Leonard and Evelyn were divorced. Leonard died recently without ever expressly revoking his will. He was survived by Evelyn, his sister, Sue, and a brother, Ted. Both of Leonard's parents died in an automobile accident three months before his death. How should Leonard's estate be distributed?

   (A) All to Evelyn.
   (B) Half to Sue and half to Ted.
   (C) All to Ted.
   (D) All to Sue.

4. One year ago, Dan, an unmarried 19-year-old who was illiterate and without issue, asked his friend to write the following:

> I, Dan Smith, do hereby declare that this is my will. I want everything I have to go to my mother. My brother, Les, is not to get anything I own.
>
> X
>
> Witnessed:
> Ben Jones...Thorp Curry

The mark "X" which appeared at the bottom of the will was made by Dan in the presence of Ben Jones and Thorp Curry, who signed as witnesses. Dan died, survived only by his brother, Les, and by his grandmother, Ann Smith. Dan's mother predeceased him by one week. How should Dan's estate be distributed?

(A) All to the estate of Dan's mother.
(B) All to Dan's grandmother, Ann Smith.
(C) Half to Dan's grandmother, Ann Smith; half to Dan's brother, Les.
(D) All to Les.

5. Ellen Morris recently died intestate. Her husband Ed had predeceased her. Ellen and Ed adopted a daughter, Lisa, and they also had a natural-born son, Tom. One year ago, Ellen gave Tom $10,000 to invest in a fast-food franchise, telling him orally that it would be deducted from his share of her estate, unless it was repaid prior to her death. A friend of Ellen was present when the conversation with Tom took place and is prepared to testify as to Ellen's statement. Ellen's net estate available for distribution is separate property of $150,000. How should her estate be distributed?

(A) $75,000 each to Lisa and Tom.
(B) $80,000 to Lisa; $70,000 to Tom.
(C) $150,000 to Tom; nothing to Lisa.
(D) $150,000 to Lisa; nothing to Tom.

6. Laura, a single woman, executed a valid will in 1990 leaving her entire estate to her mother. Two years later, she married Edward. Laura died two years after her marriage. She was survived by her mother and Edward. How should her estate be distributed?

(A) To her mother.
(B) To Edward.
(C) The first $200,000, plus three-fourths of the balance of the estate to Edward; the remaining one-fourth to her mother.
(D) The first $200,000, plus three-fourths of the balance of the estate, to her mother; the remaining one-fourth to Edward.

7. John created an *inter vivos* trust naming his children as income beneficiaries and his grandchildren as beneficiaries of the corpus. John's sister Ann then executed a valid will which contained the following bequest:

> I leave the sum of $100,000 to those persons who are the income beneficiaries, at the date of my death, under an *inter vivos* trust created by my brother, John.

At Ann's death, John had two children, Adrian and Kimberly. Ann was survived by her mother, Rita, by her brother, John, and by a sister, Lisa. How should Ann's bequest be distributed?

(A) To Adrian and Kimberly, in equal shares.

(B) To the trustee of the trust created by John with the income to be paid to Adrian and Kimberly and, at their death, the $100,000 to be paid to John's grandchildren.

(C) To Rita.

(D) One-half to Rita; one-fourth each to John and Lisa.

8. Bill executed a valid will which contained the following bequest:

> I leave the sum of $500,000 to those persons who are the residuary legatees under my mother's last will and testament.

At the time Bill executed his will, his mother had executed a valid will which left her residuary estate to Bill's uncles, Tom and Tim. Thereafter, she revoked that will and executed a new one, naming State University as her residuary legatee.

When Bill's mother died, her residuary estate was paid to State University. When Bill died, he was survived by his wife, Ann, and by one child, Emily, both of whom were provided for in his will. Bill's residuary estate was left to the American Red Cross. To whom should the $500,000 bequest be paid?

(A) To Tim and Tom, in equal shares.

(B) To State University.

(C) To the American Red Cross.

(D) To Ann as intestate property.

9. Carly executed a valid will devising her condominium to her brother Tom, and the residue of her estate to Lighthouse University, her alma mater. Several years later, Carly bought a house and entered into an installment land sales contract with Buyer for the sale of the condominium.

Carly placed the $10,000 initially paid by Buyer as a down payment on the condominium in a separate savings account entitled "Condominium Proceeds Account." All subsequent payments have also been deposited in that account.

At Carly's death, the account contained $15,000; the unpaid balance under the contract of sale was $100,000. Carly was survived by her parents and her brother Tom.

Assuming that neither the will nor the surrounding circumstances indicate anything further about how Carly would have wanted the account and the unpaid balance of the installment sales contract to be distributed, how should these two items be distributed?

(A) The account to Lighthouse University and the balance of the installment sales contract to Tom.

(B) The account and the balance of the installment sales contract to Tom.

(C) The account to Carly's parents and the balance of the installment sales contract to Tom.

(D) The account and the installment sales contract to Lighthouse University.

10. Kathy executed a valid will disposing of her entire estate. One of the dispositive provisions was as follows:

> I give all of my 100 shares of ABC Corp. stock to my good friend Edna. The remainder of my stocks, I give to my mother, Kay.

At the time the will was executed, Kathy owned exactly 100 shares of ABC Corp. stock. Shortly after execution of the will, the stock of ABC Corp. split three for one, so that Kathy now owned 300 shares. One year later, ABC Corp. declared a ten percent stock dividend so that Kathy received 30 additional shares of stock. XYZ Corp. then made a "2 for 1" tender offer for all of the outstanding shares of ABC Corp., and Kathy received 660 shares of XYZ Corp. in exchange for her ABC Corp. stock. One month later, she purchased 40 shares of XYZ Corp. for cash. Thus, at her death, Kathy owned 700 shares of XYZ Corp. stock. Kathy was survived by her son, Bill (who was alive when her will was made), her friend, Edna, and her mother, Kay.

What disposition should be made of the XYZ Corp. stock owned by Kathy at her death, assuming that the residue of the estate is devised to Bill?

(A) The XYZ Corp. stock should be distributed to Edna.

(B) One hundred shares of the XYZ Corp. stock should be distributed to Edna and the balance should be distributed to Kay.

(C) Six hundred and sixty shares of the XYZ Corp. stock should be distributed to Edna, and the balance should be distributed to Kay.

(D) All of the XYZ Corp. stock should be distributed to Bill as part of the residue of the estate.

11. Larry, a widower, executed a valid will which included the following three bequests:

> 1. I give, devise and bequeath my home to my son Ron.
>
> 2. I give, devise and bequeath the sum of $100,000 to my daughter Carolyn.
>
> 3. I give, devise and bequeath my residuary estate, in equal shares, to my son Ron and my daughter Carolyn.

At the time that Larry executed his will, he owned a home worth approximately $100,000. One year later, he conveyed this home to his son Ron, by a simple quitclaim deed that made no reference to the will. At the same time, he made a gift of $50,000 in cash to his daughter Carolyn. Shortly before his death, Larry purchased a home for $200,000, which he paid in cash. Larry recently died. His estate consists of $100,000 in cash and his home. He is survived only by Ron and Carolyn. How should his estate be distributed?

(A) To Ron and Carolyn equally.

(B) The home to Ron; the cash to Carolyn.

(C) The home to Ron and Carolyn, equally; $100,000 in cash to Carolyn.

(D) The home to Ron; $75,000 in cash to Carolyn; $25,000 in cash to Ron.

12. Bert died on July 1 from multiple gunshot wounds received in the course of a family dispute. His wife, Sofia, was convicted of murdering Bert. The conviction was affirmed on appeal. Bert left a will disposing of all of his property to Sofia, if she survived him. His estate consists of $100,000 in cash, a life insurance policy payable to Sofia as the primary beneficiary (with Bert's issue as secondary beneficiaries), and a home held in the name of Bert and Sofia as joint tenants with right of survivorship. Bert was survived by Sofia and three grandchildren. How should Bert's estate be distributed?

(A) The cash should be distributed to Sofia pursuant to the will. The insurance proceeds should be payable to Sofia pursuant to the beneficiary designation, and the joint tenancy is extinguished leaving title in Sofia alone.

(B) The cash should be distributed to the three grandchildren equally. The insurance proceeds should be payable to Sofia pursuant to the beneficiary designation, and the joint tenancy is extinguished leaving title in Sofia alone.

(C) The cash should be distributed to the three grandchildren equally. The insurance proceeds should be payable to Sofia pursuant to the beneficiary designation, and the joint tenancy is severed with the half owned by Bert passing to the three grandchildren equally.

(D) The cash and insurance proceeds should be distributed to the three grandchildren equally. The joint tenancy is severed and the half owned by Bert should pass to the three grandchildren equally.

13. Jamir executed a valid will disposing of his entire estate to his father. One year later, Jamir executed a second will which revoked the first will and disposed

of his entire estate to his mother. Six months later, Jamir tore up the second will, stating to his friend, Steve, who was present at the time, "This will take care of my estate so that my father gets it under the other will which I executed." At Jamir's death, the first will was found among his papers. He was survived by his parents and two sisters. How should Jamir's estate be distributed?

(A) To his father under the first will.

(B) To his mother under the second will.

(C) Equally, to his mother and father by intestate succession.

(D) Equally, to his sisters by intestate succession.

14. Suppose that, under the facts in Question 13, (1) Jamir's second will had provided that $1,000 was to go to his mother, with the remainder of his estate to go to his father, and (2) at the time he tore up the second will, Jamir said only, "Wills are for wimps." How should Jamir's estate be distributed?

(A) To his father under the first will.

(B) $1000 to his mother, and the remainder to his father under the second will.

(C) Equally, to his mother and father by intestate succession.

(D) Equally, to his sisters by intestate succession.

15. Edgar validly executed Will #1, which disposed of his entire estate to his brother Tom. One year later, Edgar validly executed Will #2, which disposed of his entire estate to his sister Wilma. Will #2 did not contain a revocation clause. Six months later, Edgar validly executed Will #3, which expressly revoked Will #2 and left Edgar's estate to the American Red Cross. Will #3 made no reference to Will #1. One year later, Edgar revoked Will #3 by physical act. At Edgar's death, Will #1 was found among his important papers with an unsigned note on it which read, "This is my will." Edgar was survived only by his brother Tom and his sister Wilma. How should Edgar's estate be distributed?

(A) To Tom under the terms of Will #1.

(B) To Wilma under the terms of Will #2.

(C) To The American Red Cross under the terms of Will #3.

(D) To Tom and Wilma by intestate succession.

16. Kristin executed a valid holographic will which contained the following provision:

> Within the next few days, I will prepare a list of some personal items which I wish to be given to the persons named thereon.

Several days later Kristin prepared the following handwritten list:

Mother's diamond ring — Laura; Dad's diamond stickpin — Larry; My ruby ring — Samantha

Kristin died and was survived by her children, Rusty and Rosa. Under the will, the residue of her estate, after providing for Rusty and Rosa, was given to the American Red Cross. Laura, Larry and Samantha are friends of Kristin. How should the rings and stickpin be distributed?

(A) To Laura, Larry and Samantha.

(B) To the American Red Cross as part of the residuary.

(C) To Rusty and Rosa, as part of their bequests under the will.

(D) To Rusty and Rosa under intestate principles.

17. Cary executed a valid will which made, among others, the following bequest:

> I give, devise and bequeath my grand piano to my sister, Roberta, with the hope that she will realize her dream of becoming a concert pianist.

The residue clause of Cary's will reads as follows:

> I give, devise and bequeath the remainder of my estate to my brothers and sisters, share and share alike.

At the time he executed the will, Cary had one brother, Ted, and three sisters, Roberta, Edwina and Judy. Ted predeceased Cary and was survived by his wife and one child. Roberta predeceased Ted and was survived only by her parents. Edwina and Judy survived Cary. How should Cary's estate be distributed?

(A) The piano and one-fourth of the residuary to Roberta's parents. One-fourth of the residuary each, to Edwina, Judy and Ted's child.

(B) One-third of the estate each, to Edwina, Judy and Ted's child.

(C) One-half of the estate each, to Edwina and Judy.

(D) One-sixth of the estate each, to Ted's wife and child. One-third of the estate each, to Edwina and Judy.

18. Tim executed a valid will disposing of his real estate to "my nephew Albert" and devising the remainder of his estate "to my brothers and sisters, share and share alike." Tim specifically disinherited his own children. When he died, Tim was survived by Albert, two brothers, one sister, and his (Tim's) three children. Albert has one child, a son. After Tim's death, Albert filed a valid, written statement renouncing his interest in Tim's estate. How should Tim's estate be distributed?

(A) Real estate to Albert; residue to Tim's brothers and sister.

(B) The entire estate to Tim's brothers and sister.

(C) The entire estate to Tim's children.

(D) The real estate to Albert's son; residue to Tim's two brothers and sister.

19. Tom executed a valid will disposing of "all my real estate to my sister Joan" and "the rest, residue and remainder of my estate to my brother Bill." The will also contained a provision stating that "My executor is hereby directed to pay all of my just debts." At the time Tom executed his will, he owned Blackacre, which was worth $100,000, and stock worth $100,000. One year before his death, Tom borrowed $90,000 from ABC Bank and gave the bank a mortgage on Blackacre to secure payment of the debt. He then lost all of the borrowed money gambling in Las Vegas. Blackacre is now worth $125,000 and the unpaid mortgage is still $90,000. The stock is worth $300,000. How should Tom's estate be distributed?

(A) Blackacre, encumbered by the mortgage, should be distributed to Joan; the stock should be distributed to Bill.

(B) Blackacre should be distributed to Joan free and clear of the debt; the stock remaining after payment of the debt should be distributed to Bill.

(C) Blackacre and $90,000 worth of stock should be distributed to Joan; the remainder of the stock should be distributed to Bill.

(D) Since Tom's testamentary scheme was to treat Joan and Bill equally, Blackacre and the stock should be sold, the debt to ABC Bank paid and the remainder distributed equally to Joan and Bill.

20. John and Betty met in Hawaii, where both were vacationing. They spent much of their time together. After they returned to their homes, Betty discovered that she was pregnant. After her child, Jennifer, was born, Betty, who had never married John, sued John to establish paternity. Although John denied that Jennifer was his child, the jury found by clear and convincing evidence that John was the father. The court entered judgment accordingly. Thereafter, John refused to acknowledge Jennifer as his child or to spend any time with her, but did pay the support ordered by the court. When John died, his will (executed prior to the birth of Jennifer) left his entire estate to ABC Charity. John was survived by Betty, Jennifer and his parents. How should his estate be distributed?

(A) To Jennifer.

(B) To ABC Charity.

(C) Half to Jennifer, and the remainder to ABC Charity.

(D) Half to Jennifer, and the remainder to John's parents, in equal shares.

21. Suppose that, in Question 20, Jennifer was the one who died, and that she was survived by her mother, Betty, her father, John, and two sisters. Assume further that Betty married John after the paternity suit described in Question

20, and the sisters were conceived by Betty during that marriage to John. If Jennifer died without a will, how should her estate be distributed?

(A) To John and Betty, equally.
(B) To Betty.
(C) One-half to Betty; the other one-half to Jennifer's sisters.
(D) To Jennifer's sisters in equal shares.

22. Jane had two children, Will and Mark, by her first marriage. After the death of her first husband, she remarried and had one child, Kane, by her second husband, Steve. Jane then died. One year later, Mark died intestate. Mark was survived only by Will and Kane. Steve is still alive. How should Mark's estate be distributed?

(A) To Will.
(B) To Will and Kane, in equal shares.
(C) One-third each to Steve, Will and Kane.
(D) One-half to Steve; one-fourth each to Will and Kane.

23. Ted died in an automobile accident. He was survived by his wife Judy and theirdaughter Lisa. Judy has a child, Amy, by reason of an earlier marriage. Shortly after Ted's death, Judy discovered that she was two months pregnant. Judy gave birth to a son, Ted, Jr. seven months after Ted's death. Assuming that Ted died intestate, how should his estate be distributed?

(A) The first $150,000, plus one-half of the balance of the intestate estate to Judy; the remaining one-half to Lisa.
(B) The first $150,000, plus one-half of the balance of the intestate estate to Judy; the remaining one-half to be divided between Lisa and Ted, Jr., equally.
(C) One-half of the intestate estate to Judy; the remaining one-half to be divided between Lisa and Ted, Jr., equally.
(D) One-half of the intestate estate to Judy; the remaining one-half to Lisa.

24. Suppose that, in Question 23, Lisa and Amy were Ted's children by reason of an earlier marriage, and that only Ted, Jr. was the child of both Ted and Judy. How should Ted's estate be distributed?

(A) The first $100,000, plus one-half of the balance of the intestate estate to Judy; the remaining one-half to be divided among Lisa, Amy and Ted, Jr., equally.
(B) The first $100,000, plus one-half of the balance of the intestate estate to Judy; the remaining one-half to be divided between Lisa and Amy, equally.

(C) One-half of the intestate estate to Judy; the remaining one-half to be divided among Lisa, Amy and Ted, Jr., equally.

(D) One-half of the intestate estate to Judy; the remaining one-half to be divided between Lisa and Amy, equally.

25. When Lisa was seven years old, her parents were killed in an automobile accident. The night of the accident, her aunt and uncle, Harvey and Ann, arrived and told Lisa that she was going to go live with them and "be our little girl." Several years later, they told Lisa, "You're going to court with us, so that you can be our little girl forever." Harvey and Ann held Lisa out as their daughter. She participated in every way as a member of their family. Harvey had a son, Bob, by reason of a previous marriage. When Harvey died intestate, Ann claimed his entire estate. After consulting an attorney, Lisa found out that, while Harvey and Ann had obtained legal custody of her, there had been no formal adoption. Harvey was survived by Ann, Lisa, Bob and Harvey's parents. How should his estate be distributed?

(A) The first $200,000, plus three-quarters of the balance of the estate to Ann; the remaining one-quarter of the estate to Harvey's parents.

(B) The first $100,000, plus one-half of the balance of the intestate estate to Ann; the remaining one-half to be divided between Bob and Lisa, equally.

(C) One-half of the intestate estate to Ann; the remaining one-half to be divided between Bob and Lisa, equally.

(D) The entire intestate estate to Ann.

26. Patricia was preparing for a trip to the Caribbean. She wrote the following and signed it in her own handwriting:

> I am getting ready to take a cruise. If I don't return from the cruise, I want my entire estate to go to the County Art Museum.
> /s/ Patricia

Patricia took the cruise and returned. One month later, she died. She was survived by her mother and a brother. How should her estate be distributed?

(A) To her mother, because the holographic will was not dated.

(B) To her mother and brother, equally.

(C) To the County Art Museum.

(D) One-half each to the County Art Museum and her mother.

27. Arnold and his father, Clay, orally agreed that Clay could live in Arnold's house, that Arnold would provide Clay with food and clothing, and that Clay would make a will leaving his entire estate to Arnold at Clay's death. When Clay died, he left a valid will which (1) made no reference to the agreement with Arnold, and (2) disposed of his entire estate to Anne. How should Clay's

estate be distributed, assuming (1) Clay was survived by Arnold and Arnold's brother, Tom, and (2) Anne also wishes to take the estate?

(A) Anne.

(B) Arnold.

(C) Arnold and Tom, equally.

(D) One-half to Anne and one-half to Arnold and Tom, equally.

28. Suppose that, in Question 27, Arnold and Clay had put their agreement in writing and that Clay moved into Arnold's home and has lived there until the present. (For this question only, assume that Clay is still alive.) Several years ago, after signing the agreement, Clay transferred one-half of his assets to Tom. What remedy, if any, can Arnold obtain against Clay or Tom, while Clay is still alive?

(A) Specific performance to require Tom to transfer the assets to Arnold.

(B) Anticipatory breach of the agreement, with damages paid to Arnold.

(C) An injunction preventing Clay from transferring his assets and requiring Tom to reconvey the assets to Clay.

(D) Anticipatory breach of the agreement, with a constructive trust being imposed upon the assets transferred to Tom.

29. Two years before her death, Toni, a widow, executed a valid will in which she gave her entire estate to her church, First Baptist. At her death, the will could not be found. Her attorney, Agnes, has a conformed copy of the will and can testify that she had a conversation with Toni the week before her death in which Toni affirmed that her will, as executed, still represented her testamentary wishes. Toni was survived by her two children, Rob and Adam, both of whom were born prior to the making of the will, and her parents. To whom is it likely that the estate will be distributed?

(A) To the First Baptist Church.

(B) Half of the estate to the First Baptist Church; half to Rob and Adam, equally.

(C) To Rob and Adam.

(D) Half of the estate to Toni's parents; half to Rob and Adam, equally.

30. Parker, a widower, executed a valid will which disposed of his entire estate to "the children of my best friend, Sam Riley." At the time the will was executed and at Parker's death, Sam Riley had no children. After Parker's death, Sam had three children, Bob, Sally, and Ellen. Parker was survived by his sister, Ann, and his parents. To whom should Parker's estate be distributed?

(A) To Bob, as Sam's first-born child.

(B) To Bob, Sally and Ellen, at Sam's death.

(C) To Ann.

(D) To Parker's parents.

31. Suppose that, in Question 30, the gift was "to the children of my best friend, Sam Riley" and that at the time Parker died, (1) Bob, Sam's eldest child, was already alive, and (2) Sally and Ellen were born after Parker's death. To whom should Parker's estate be distributed?

(A) To Bob.

(B) To Bob, Sally and Ellen.

(C) To Ann.

(D) To Parker's parents.

32. Suppose that, in Question 30, the gift was "to the children of my best friend, Sam Riley, who reach the age of 25." When Parker died, Bob, the eldest child, was 15. Prior to Bob's reaching age 25, Ellen was born. Sally was born after Bob reached age 25. How should Parker's estate be distributed?

(A) To Bob.

(B) One-half each to be held for Bob and Ellen until they reach age 25, and then paid to them; but if either dies before reaching age 25, remainder to the one who survives.

(C) One-third to Bob; remainder to be held until Ellen and Sally reach age 25, and then distributed to them equally. If they fail to reach age 25, the remainder to be split among the other members of the class who reach age 25.

(D) One-third to Bob, Ellen and Sally, immediately.

33. Suppose that, in Question 30, the only gift was "$10,000 each to the children of my best friend, Sam Riley" and that at the time Parker died, Sam Riley had no children. Bob, Sally and Ellen were born after Parker's death. To whom should Parker's estate be distributed (assuming that the will made no other gifts)?

(A) $10,000 to Bob; one-half of the remainder to Ann; the balance to Parker's parents.

(B) $10,000 each to Bob, Sally and Ellen; the balance to Parker's parents.

(C) To Parker's parents.

(D) To Ann, entirely.

34. Edward and Mary validly executed joint and reciprocal wills in which each disposed of his or her property to the survivor; upon the death of the survivor, all property was to go to their children. Mary died, her will was probated and her property was distributed to Edward. Thereafter, Edward executed another valid will, leaving all of his property to his friend, Ann. When Edward died, he was survived by one child, Tim, and by two grandchildren who were the issue of Lisa, the predeceased daughter of Edward and Mary. How should Edward's estate be distributed?

(A) One-half to Tim, and one-fourth each to the grandchildren pursuant to Edward's original will.

(B) One-half to Tim, and one-fourth each to the grandchildren by intestate succession.

(C) All to Tim by intestate succession.

(D) All to Ann.

35. Bill executed a last will and testament. It made two bequests, as follows:

1. $10,000 to my son, Jim.

2. All the rest, residue and remainder of my estate to my daughter, Elizabeth.

The will also explicitly revoked a prior valid will which had expressly disinherited Jim and left everything to Elizabeth. Bill was survived by his two children (Jim and Elizabeth) and his parents. It is admitted by all parties that Bill's first will was valid. Assuming that there are grounds for opposing the probate of Bill's second will, who may contest probate of the will?

(A) Jim only.

(B) Jim or Elizabeth.

(C) Jim or Elizabeth or Bill's parents.

(D) Elizabeth only.

36. John and Beth Askew were married for many years. During the course of their marriage, a son, Clay, was born. Clay was the only child John ever had. Although he had no rational basis for his suspicions, John believed that Clay was conceived as the result of a relationship between Beth and another man. Although Beth denied this, John persisted in his belief. Several tests showed that Clay had the same blood type as John. Beth died when Clay was four. When Clay was six, John executed a holographic will (the only will he ever made), reading as follows:

> My wife has betrayed me. She gave birth to a child by another man. The child is not mine, although I have provided a home for him. I therefore disinherit Clay. I leave everything to my aunt, Matilda Askew.
>
> /s/John Askew

John died without changing his belief or the will. Should the will be admitted to probate?

(A) No, if John was suffering from an insane delusion.

(B) Yes, if the will was validly executed.

(C) No, since John had been unduly influenced in his beliefs.

(D) Yes, since John has the absolute right to disinherit his son.

37. Assume the same facts described in Question 36, except that (1) there was a rational basis for John's belief that Clay was the product of an illicit relationship, and (2) the final sentence of John's holographic will (leaving everything to Aunt Matilda) was omitted.

John died without changing (1) his belief that Clay was the product of an illicit relationship, or (2) the purported will. Should the document be admitted to probate?

(A) No, because the purported will is not a valid testamentary document.

(B) No, because a natural father cannot disinherit his son.

(C) Yes, because the writing constitutes a valid holographic will.

(D) No, because John's belief about Clay's parentage was mistaken, although rational.

38. Fred Jones, an attorney, had represented Ellen Morris for many years. Ellen requested that Jones prepare a will for her and that a bequest of $10,000 to Jones be included in the will. Jones, sensing that it would be improper for him to draw a will in which he was a legatee, asked his associate Michael Fox to prepare the will. Fox did so and returned the will to Jones for execution by Ellen. When Ellen died, Jones filed an application to probate the will. Assuming that Ellen's son, Thad, who received the residue of the estate, wishes to contest the will, upon what basis is he most likely to be successful?

(A) Undue influence.

(B) Fraud.

(C) Lack of testamentary capacity.

(D) Violation of the Rules of Professional Conduct applicable to lawyers.

39. Robin Thomas was married to Hal Thomas. One month after they agreed to a "trial" separation, Robin met Craig Jones (a very wealthy businessman) at a bar in another city. When Craig proposed to Robin two months later, Robin accepted. When Robin and Craig applied for a marriage license, Robin represented that she was single. One week after they were married, Craig signed a valid will which left one-half of his estate to "My beloved wife, Robin," and one-half to his Aunt Martha. In his will, Craig explicitly stated that although he had two children from a previous marriage, he wanted them to receive nothing (because they had sided with his previous wife). Aunt Martha, however, had stood by him.

Craig died one month later, survived by Robin, Aunt Martha and his two children. His children requested that the will be denied probate. What action is the court likely to take?

(A) Admit the will to probate, since Craig can leave his estate to whomever he wishes.

(B) Admit the will to probate, but impose a constructive trust upon Robin's share in favor of Aunt Martha.

(C) Deny the will to probate, since it was procured by fraud.

(D) Deny the will to probate, since Craig was mistaken as to Robin's marital status.

40. John executed a will giving his friend, Ted, a power of appointment over the residue of John's estate. The residuary clause reads as follows:

> I give, devise and bequeath the rest, residue and remainder of my estate to such person or persons as my friend, Ted, may appoint either by deed during Ted's lifetime or by his will; if my friend, Ted, does not exercise this power of appointment, at Ted's death the residue of my estate shall be distributed to my heirs.

The power of appointment given to Ted is classified as a:

(A) General power presently exercisable.

(B) Special power presently exercisable.

(C) General testamentary power.

(D) Special testamentary power.

41. Suppose that, in Question 40, Ted fails to exercise the power during his life, but executes a will which disposes of his property as follows:

> I give $10,000 to my only son, Bill. All the rest, residue and remainder of my estate, I give to my wife, Ann.

How should the property over which Ted was given a power of appointment under John's will be distributed?

(A) To Ann.

(B) The first $50,000, plus one-half of the balance to Ann; the remainder to Bill.

(C) To John's heirs.

(D) To Ted's heirs.

42. Suppose that, in Question 40, at the time he executed his will, John had three children, Art, Bob and Charles. Art died before John without a spouse or issue. Art left a will devising all his property to the American Red Cross. At John's death, Bob and Charles were living; however, both predeceased Ted.

Bob left no issue, but was survived by his wife, Sally, to whom he left his entire estate by will. Charles was survived by his wife, Marcy, to whom he left his entire estate by will, and by one child, Ned.

Assuming that Ted failed to exercise the power of appointment (during his lifetime or by his will), how should the property be distributed?

(A) One-third to the American Red Cross; one-third to Sally; one-third to Marcy.

(B) One-half to Sally; one-half to Marcy.

(C) One-half to Marcy; one-half to Ned.

(D) All to Ned.

43. Suppose that, in Question 40, Ted exercised the power of appointment by his will, and that the main provision read as follows:

> I give, devise and bequeath the property over which I have a power of appointment to John's children, Art, Bob and Charles, in equal shares.

Suppose further that (1) all of John's children predeceased Ted, and (2) none of them left surviving spouses or issue. The residuary clause of Ted's will left all of his property to his wife, Ann. Ted was survived by Ann and Bill, his son by reason of a previous marriage. John's only heirs were his two brothers. How should the property which was subject to Ted's power be distributed?

(A) To John's brothers, in equal shares.

(B) To Ann.

(C) The first $100,000, plus one-half of the balance, to Ann; the remainder to Bill.

(D) To Bill.

Questions 44-47 are based upon the following fact situation:

Ten years ago, T purchased 300 shares of the stock of Rex, Inc., a family corporation. Nine years ago, T executed a valid will, which provided as follows:

(1) I give 300 shares of Rex, Inc. stock and $1,000 to my brother-in-law Ben.

(2) I give the sum of $15,000 to my son Mike.

(3) I give the residue of my estate to my wife Doris.

Liz, T's second child (by Doris), was born after T executed his will and on the very day T was seriously injured in a heated altercation with his brother-in-law, Ben. T subsequently sold his Rex stock for $15,000 and invested the proceeds in municipal bonds.

Doris obtained a valid final judgment of divorce from T nine months ago. T married Kay six months ago.

One week ago, T died as a result of the injuries he received in the altercation with Ben. Ben was arrested for voluntary manslaughter, tried and convicted.

T's estate, entirely his separate property, consisted of the municipal bonds now worth $20,000 and cash of $110,000 on deposit at City Bank. T is survived by Ben, Mike, Liz, Kay and Doris.

44. How much of T's estate will Doris receive?

 (A) One-half.
 (B) The entire estate, less the gifts to Mike and Ben.
 (C) Nothing.
 (D) None of the above.

45. How much of T's estate will Kay receive?

 (A) One-half.
 (B) The entire estate, less the gifts to Mike and Ben.
 (C) Nothing.
 (D) None of the above.

46. How much of T's estate will Liz receive?

 (A) One-fourth.
 (B) One-third.
 (C) Nothing.
 (D) None of the above.

47. How much of T's estate will Ben receive?

 (A) Nothing, because the gifts to Ben were adeemed by extinction.
 (B) Nothing, because he killed T.
 (C) The value of the stock when it was sold, plus $1,000.
 (D) $21,000 (the value of the bonds at T's death, plus $1,000).

48. Ralph devised property to Sam in trust to pay the income to Linda for life, and on Linda's death to distribute the principal to such of Linda's issue as Linda should appoint by will. If Linda did not exercise the power of appointment, at Linda's death Sam was to distribute the principal to Linda's then living issue, the issue to take per stirpes.

Prior to Linda's death, she delivered a written letter to Sam stating that she released all rights which she might have as donee of the power of appointment which Ralph had given to her. Thereafter, Linda executed a will which disposed of all property which she owned, including any property "over which I hold a power of appointment," to her son, Adam. When Linda died, she was survived by two children, Adam and Ron, and by a grandchild, Martha, the issue of a predeceased daughter, Karen. How should Sam distribute that part of Ralph's property subject to appointment?

(A) To Adam, Ron and Martha, in equal shares.

(B) To Adam.

(C) To Adam and Ron, in equal shares.

(D) To Ralph's heirs.

49. Suppose that, in Question 48, prior to Linda's death, she entered into a contract with Adam, one of her children. The terms of the agreement were that, in exchange for the payment of $10,000 to Linda by Adam, Linda agreed to exercise the power of appointment in favor of Adam. Adam paid the $10,000. However, at Linda's death, her will provided for exercise of the power in favor of Adam, Ron, and Martha, equally. How should the court distribute the property?

(A) To Adam, pursuant to the contract.

(B) To Adam and Ron, equally, as Linda's children.

(C) To Adam, Ron and Martha, pursuant to the exercise of the power.

(D) To Adam, Ron and Martha, as takers in default of the power.

50. Alice transferred $1,000,000 to her brother Jim; the transfer was carried out without any statement of conditions by Alice. Two weeks later, Alice told Jim, "That $1,000,000 I gave you is to be held by you for the benefit of all of my children. If you don't agree, I want it all back." Jim responded by telling Alice, "You gave me that money, I'll use it the way you want me to." Alice later heard that Jim had told other people that he wasn't going to give Alice's children a penny. Alice filed suit against Jim to recover the money, but died before the case came to trial. Assume that:

(1) Alice died survived by two children, Bill and Penny, and

(2) Alice's will left everything to Bill and Penny.

How should the court order distribution of the money?

(A) To Jim, outright.

(B) To Penny, outright.

(C) To Jim in trust for Bill and Penny.

(D) To Bill and Penny, outright.

51. Stephanie executed a will which gave all her property to her son Rick. Thereafter, she wrote and delivered to her brother, Sam, a letter which reads as follows:

> Dear Sam: As you know, I am leaving for Europe in two weeks. When I return, it is my intent that my farm, on which you now reside, shall be placed in trust for the benefit of your children. I have given the rest of my estate to Rick. All my love, Stephanie.

Stephanie died while on her European trip. She was survived by Sam, Sam's daughter, Tina, Stephanie's mother Ann, and Rick. How should the court dispose of the farm?

(A) Since a valid trust was created upon delivery of the letter to Sam, the farm should be distributed to Sam as trustee for Tina.

(B) No valid trust was created, and so the farm should be distributed to Rick pursuant to the will.

(C) Although no valid trust was created at the time of delivery of the letter, a trust came into being upon Stephanie's death, and so the property should be distributed to Sam as trustee for Tina.

(D) No valid trust was created, and so the farm should be distributed to Rick under intestacy principles.

52. Ralph gave property to Sam in trust. Sam was directed to pay the income to Linda for life, and on Linda's death to distribute the principal to any one or more of Linda's issue as Linda should appoint by her will. If Linda did not exercise the power of appointment, at Linda's death Sam was to distribute the principal to Linda's then living issue, by right of representation. The power of appointment bestowed upon Linda is:

(A) A general power, presently exercisable.

(B) A general testamentary power.

(C) A special power, presently exercisable.

(D) A special testamentary power.

53. Christina executed a valid will which made the following bequest:

> I give, devise and bequeath to my friend, John, as trustee, the sum of $15,000. I direct that he invest this money and, once each year, use the income therefrom to throw a party for the persons who are my three best friends at the time of my death.

At Christina's death, John advised the court that he was willing to carry out the terms of the trust. He also stated that it was unclear who Christina's three best friends were at the time of her death, but that if he had to guess, he'd say that they were Ann, Barbara and Cary. The residue of Christina's estate was bequeathed to her mother. How should the court distribute Christina's estate?

(A) Fifteen thousand dollars to John, as trustee to be used for the purpose stated in the will; remainder of the estate to Christina's mother.

(B) Fifteen thousand dollars to John, as trustee of a trust for *all* of Christina's friends; remainder of the estate to Christina's mother.

(C) Five thousand dollars each, to Ann, Barbara and Cary; remainder of the estate to Christina's mother.

(D) All to Christina's mother.

54. T was feeling very weak. After T signed her typed will in front of X and Y, Y left the room to obtain a glass of water for T. While Y was away, X signed the will as a witness. When Y returned, she signed the will in front of X and T. Which of the following statements is correct?

(A) T has a valid holographic will.

(B) T has a valid formal will.

(C) T's will is invalid, because the witnesses did not sign in each other's presence.

(D) T's will is invalid, if the will was undated.

55. T was in a hospital, feeling increasingly weak. T announced to X and Y that the document which he was about to ask them to witness was a will. After T signed the typewritten will, he began to cough continuously. Dr. Debbie rushed into T's hospital room and asked X and Y to leave. They left the room and signed T's will as witnesses in the hospital lobby. Which of the following statements is correct?

(A) T has a valid holographic will.

(B) T has a valid formal will.

(C) T's will is not valid, because the witnesses did not sign in his presence.

(D) T's will is not valid, if X and Y did not actually read the document.

56. Bruce made the following bequest in his will:

> I give, devise, and bequeath the sum of $10,000 to my friend, Selma, as trustee, the income and such portion of the corpus as may be necessary to be used by her to provide care and shelter for my dog, Rusty.

The remainder of Bruce's property was bequeathed to the Humane Society in the city where Bruce lived. At Bruce's death, Selma declared that she was willing to carry out the terms of Bruce's trust. How would Bruce's estate be distributed in most U.S. jurisdictions?

    (A) Ten thousand dollars to Selma to be held in trust for Rusty; the remainder to the Humane Society.

    (B) Ten thousand dollars to Selma free of trust; the remainder to the Humane Society.

    (C) All to the Humane Society.

    (D) None of the above.

57. Elaine made the following bequest in her will:

> I give, devise and bequeath the sum of $1,000,000 to my husband, Will, if he survives me, as trustee, the income from such trust to be paid to my husband so long as he remains unmarried. In the event that my husband shall remarry, or upon his death, whichever shall first occur, I appoint my brother, Tom, as successor trustee, to pay the income to my children, so long as they remain unmarried. In the event they marry, or upon their deaths, whichever first occurs, to pay all accrued income and principal to my alma mater, State College.

Elaine was survived by her husband, Will, her brother, Tom, and her children, Bob and Ellen. Will, Bob and Ellen have petitioned the court to strike the conditions that they not marry and distribute the property in other respects in accordance with the trust. How should the court distribute Elaine's estate?

    (A) The court should strike the conditions as to all beneficiaries and distribute $1,000,000 to Will, as trustee.

    (B) The court should strike the conditions as to Will, but not as to Bob and Ellen and distribute $1,000,000 to Will, as trustee.

    (C) The court should strike the conditions as to Bob and Ellen, but not as to Will, and distribute $1,000,000 to Will as trustee.

    (D) The court should declare the trust invalid and distribute the property pursuant to the residuary clause of the will, or by intestate succession, whichever is appropriate.

58. Judith made an unconditional bequest of $200,000 in her will to her brother, Earl. The bequest was preceded by a conversation between Judith and Earl, in which Earl agreed to hold the property in trust for Judith's friend, Grace. The residue of Judith's estate was bequeathed to her "brothers and sisters, in equal shares." At Judith's death, Earl advised Grace, as well as his brothers and sisters, that the $200,000 was his, outright. Judith was survived by Grace, Earl, one other brother and two sisters. What of the following should guide the court in regard to the bequest to Earl?

    (A) The oral agreement to hold the funds in trust is enforceable by Grace as an express trust.

    (B) The oral agreement to hold the funds in trust is enforceable by Grace as a constructive trust.

(C) The oral agreement to hold the funds in trust should be enforced as a resulting trust by Judith's brothers and sisters.

(D) The bequest passes to Earl alone.

59. Suppose that, in Question 58, the bequest by Judith in her will was to "my brother, Earl, in trust for someone mentioned to him during my lifetime." If Earl refuses to perform the trust, what action should the court take in regard to the bequest to Earl?

(A) The oral agreement to hold the property in trust may be enforced as an express trust by Grace.

(B) The oral agreement to hold the property in trust may be enforced as a constructive trust by Grace.

(C) The oral agreement to hold the property in trust may be enforced as a resulting trust by Judith's brothers and sisters.

(D) The bequest passes to Earl, outright.

60. Amy Jones deposited $10,000 in a bank account at First Bank. The account was created as "Amy Jones, Trustee for Karen Smith." Karen Smith is Amy's friend. Amy used this account as her checking account, depositing her monthly paychecks into the account and paying her bills from it. Karen Smith had no knowledge of the account. After creating this account, Amy executed a will in which she left all of her property to her brother, Ed Jones. Amy recently died and was survived by her parents, her friend, Karen, and her brothers, Ed and Warren Jones. The balance in the account at Amy's death was $35,000. How should the bank account be distributed?

(A) To Karen Smith.

(B) To Ed Jones.

(C) To Karen, Ed and Warren, in equal shares.

(D) To Amy's parents, in equal shares.

61. Suppose that, in Question 60, Karen Smith predeceased Amy Jones, and that (1) Amy never changed the designation on the bank account, and (2) Karen was survived by her daughter, LeeAnn, and her husband Mike Smith. Suppose further that Karen, after the birth of LeeAnn, executed a valid will disposing of all of her property to her husband Mike. How should the bank account be distributed?

(A) To Mike Smith.

(B) To LeeAnn.

(C) To Ed Jones.

(D) To Amy's parents, in equal shares.

62. Able created a revocable *inter vivos* trust with Blackacre (a farm) as the trust res, Baker as the trustee, and Carl as the beneficiary. Baker, as trustee, was directed to pay the income from the trust (*i.e.,* profits from operation of the farm) to Carl, until Carl reached age 45, and then to deed Blackacre to Carl in fee simple absolute. The trust contained no statement regarding Carl's right to alienate his interest in the trust. Carl, in order to satisfy a debt he owed to Sam, made a written assignment of "all my right, title and interest in Blackacre" to Sam. Under these circumstances:

(A) Sam acquires no interest in Blackacre.

(B) Sam acquires a right to the income interest only.

(C) Sam may require the trust to terminate, and Baker to convey Blackacre to him (since Carl no longer owns any interest in the property).

(D) Sam may require the trustee to pay the income to him until Carl reaches age 45, and then to deed Blackacre to him when Carl reaches age 45.

63. Suppose that, in Question 62, subsequent to the assignment to Sam, (1) Carl assigned his interest in the trust to Ted, and, (2) Ted was the first to notify Baker of the assignment. As between Sam and Ted, who has the greater right?

(A) Sam, since the first assignment has priority.

(B) Sam, but only if Sam gave present consideration in exchange for the transfer.

(C) Ted, since the first assignee to notify the trustee of his assignment prevails.

(D) Ted, if he gave present consideration for the transfer.

64. Lucille is the life income beneficiary of a trust created by her mother. The trust res includes Blackacre. Lucille receives quarterly distributions of income from the trust. At her death, the remainder interest in the trust will go to her children. However, Lucille is presently unmarried and has no children. Caleb obtained a final judgment against Lucille arising out of an automobile accident in which Caleb was injured. The marshal has delivered a writ of execution to the trustee of Lucille's trust. Under these circumstances:

(A) The writ of execution, a legal remedy, is ineffective against an equitable interest in the trust.

(B) The marshal may order Blackacre sold at public sale in satisfaction of Caleb's judgment. The remainder of the proceeds, if any, would then be returned to the trustee.

(C) The trustee must pay the income to the marshal for application against the judgment until it is fully satisfied or Lucille dies, whichever occurs first.

(D) The trustee must deed Blackacre to Caleb, outright.

65. Alice created a trust in her will which provides that the income shall be paid to her children during their lifetimes, and upon the death of her last child, the principal shall be divided among her grandchildren. The trust contains the following clause:

> My children shall not, by way of present or future anticipation, assign their interest in this trust under any circumstances. The income interest of my children shall not be subject to the claims of their creditors, whether by voluntary or involuntary transfer.

After Alice's death, one of her children, Beatrix, directed that her income installments be paid to her sister, Karen, in satisfaction of a debt which Beatrix owed to Karen. Under these circumstances:

(A) The transfer of Beatrix's income interest is void.

(B) The transfer of Beatrix's income interest is valid, and the trustee must pay Beatrix's income interest to Karen.

(C) The transfer of Beatrix's income interest is valid, but revocable by Beatrix; and so the trustee may pay the income to Karen until Beatrix revokes the assignment.

(D) Although the transfer of Beatrix's income is void, the debt owed to Karen by Beatrix is deemed to be satisfied, because Karen knew the transfer was void.

66. Suppose that, in Question 65, the United States obtained a judgment against Beatrix for unpaid income taxes. Under these circumstances:

(A) The judgment of the United States takes priority over a spendthrift clause, and the trustee must pay the income to the United States.

(B) The judgment of the United States takes priority over a spendthrift clause, and the trustee must deliver principal sufficient to satisfy Beatrix's income tax delinquency to the United States.

(C) The spendthrift clause is valid against the judgment of the United States; but, the trustee may pay the income to the United States until Beatrix objects.

(D) The spendthrift clause is valid against the judgment of the United States, and so the trustee may not pay any of Beatrix's income to the United States.

67. John, a widower, made the following bequest in his valid will:

> I give, devise and bequeath the sum of $1,000,000 to my friend, Ted, in the hope that he will use such funds for his children.

At the time that John made the bequest, Ted had two children, Andy and Lon. John's will gave his residuary estate to his father, Bill. John was survived by

Bill. Ted contends that he has no obligation to use any of the money for the benefit of his children. What action, if any, should the court take in relation to this gift?

(A) It should declare the property to be held in trust for Ted's children, remove Ted as trustee and appoint a successor trustee.

(B) It should find a resulting trust in favor of John's father, Bill.

(C) It should find a constructive trust in favor of John's father, Bill.

(D) It should declare the property to belong to Ted outright.

68. In her will, Kathy created a trust by transferring stocks and bonds worth $1,000,000 to National Bank as trustee, for the following purpose:

> The trustee shall distribute to my grandchildren such amounts of income as it, in its sole and complete discretion, shall determine is necessary for their care, education, maintenance and support. At the death of the last of my children to die, the trustee shall distribute all unpaid income and the principal of this trust to my grandchildren then living, per capita.

After Kathy's death (but before the death of her children) one of Kathy's grandchildren, (Larry), incurred a debt which he could not pay. The creditor obtained a judgment against Larry. Under these circumstances:

(A) The creditor may levy against Larry's income interest in the hands of the trustee.

(B) The creditor may obtain a lien against (but not a sale of) Larry's remainder interests in the hands of the trustee.

(C) The creditor may levy against Larry's income and remainder interests in the hands of the trustee.

(D) The creditor may not levy against Larry's income or remainder interests in the hands of the trustee.

69. Ted created an *inter vivos* trust by transferring $500,000 to First National Bank, as trustee. The declaration of trust provided that the income of the trust was to be paid to Ted during his lifetime. At his death, the principal was to be distributed to Ted's daughter, Mae. The trust provides as follows:

> No beneficiary of this trust may, by way of present or future anticipation, assign his or her interest in this trust, under any circumstance. The income interest of any beneficiary shall not be subject to the claims of creditors, whether by way of voluntary or involuntary transfer.

Several years after this trust was created, Ron obtained a judgment against Ted in the sum of $400,000. This obligation arose after the trust was created. Under these circumstances:

(A) The income interest of Ted is exempt from his creditors.

(B) Ron may not levy on Ted's interest in the hands of the trustee, but may levy on any income actually received by Ted.

(C) Ron may levy on Ted's income interest, but not on the remainder interest.

(D) Ron may levy on both the income and remainder interests

70. Leslie created a trust of $250,000, with The First Bank as trustee, for the following purpose:

> The principal of this trust, together with all accrued income therefrom, shall be paid over to the person who discovers a cure for cancer.

This trust is:

(A) Valid, because its purpose is to promote medical research.

(B) Invalid, because it will benefit a limited number of persons.

(C) Invalid, because it is not certain to vest within the allowable period of the Rule Against Perpetuities.

(D) Invalid, because it is not certain ever to vest.

71. Suppose that, in Question 70, the trust had the following purpose:

> The principal of this trust, together with all accrued income therefrom, shall be used for charitable purposes.

This trust is:

(A) Invalid, because the beneficiaries are unascertainable.

(B) Invalid, because the trust violates the Rule Against Perpetuities.

(C) Valid, with the trustee authorized to pay over the proceeds to any charity which the trustor had supported during his lifetime.

(D) Valid, with the trustee authorized to use the trust funds to support any recognized charity.

72. Lynn created a testamentary trust which provides as follows:

> I give, devise and bequeath the sum of $1,000,000 in trust to First National Bank, as Trustee. The trustee shall pay from the income the sum of $100 to each person who is convicted of possession but has less than one ounce of marijuana. It is my belief that this law is an unconstitutional invasion of privacy and that these people should not suffer for their transgression. Perhaps this trust will wake our legislators up to the need for a revision of the law. The trustee shall have the sole and exclusive right to ascertain which persons should receive payments from the trust income.

Lynn was survived by her son, Max, to whom she devised the residue of her estate. Under these circumstances:

(A) The trust may be sustained as a valid charitable trust for the promotion of health.

(B) The trust may be sustained as a valid charitable trust for the advancement of education.

(C) The trust may be sustained as a valid trust for general charitable purposes.

(D) The trust is invalid as a charitable trust and the trust res should be distributed to Max.

73. Maura created a testamentary trust which provides as follows:

> I give, devise and bequeath the sum of $1,000,000 in trust to First National Bank, trustee; the income therefrom to be paid to International University to provide scholarships for children of low-income families.

International University is a privately-owned, profit-making corporation which educates persons for technical jobs in industry. It has an outstanding reputation.

Maura was survived by her son, Will, to whom she devised the remainder of her estate. Under these circumstances:

(A) The trust is a valid charitable trust for education.

(B) The trust is a valid charitable trust to mitigate poverty.

(C) The trust is a valid charitable trust, only if the recipients of the scholarships are indigent.

(D) The trust is invalid as a charitable trust, and so the trust property should be distributed to Will.

74. Terry created a testamentary trust which provides as follows:

> I give, devise and bequeath the sum of $500,000 to my alma mater, Normal University, the income therefrom to be used to provide scholarships for worthy students from the state of Arizona.

Terry was a graduate of Normal University. After Terry's will was executed, Normal University ceased to operate as a university. Its facilities were sold to Welcome University, a privately-owned, profit-making school. Terry devised the remainder of her estate to her parents. Terry died recently. Under these circumstances:

(A) The charitable gift should be distributed to Welcome University.

(B) The charitable gift should be distributed to another non-profit university chosen by the court.

(C) The charitable gift should fail and be distributed to Terry's parents.

(D) The charitable gift should fail and be distributed to Terry's heirs.

75. Settlor made a testamentary, charitable gift of $1,000,000 to Delphi University for the following purposes:

> The income from this gift shall be used to provide scholarships for the education of white, male students at Delphi University who regularly attend their respective churches, temples or synagogues. Women, and minority students probably receive sufficient aid already. I do not wish to spend my money on atheists.

Delphi is a non-profit, non-sectarian, coeducational institution. It has prided itself on educating disadvantaged persons, regardless of race or creed. It desperately needs money to provide additional scholarships for its students. However, Delphi is prohibited by its charter from accepting a gift with racial restrictions. Settlor recently died. Under these circumstances a court would probably:

(A) Strike all of the restrictions, and sustain the entire gift to Delphi.

(B) Substitute another institution which can adhere to the restrictions.

(C) Strike the racial restriction only, and sustain the gift to Delphi with the other restrictions attached.

(D) Void the gift and distribute the funds to the residuary legatees or trustor's heirs.

76. Edward is the trustee of an *inter vivos* trust created by his father. The trust res consists of an office building which produces revenue that is equivalent to a 4.5% return on investment. In order to increase income resulting from the trust, Edward purchased the office building from the trust for $200,000 and caused the trust to invest the proceeds in higher-yield assets. The trust instrument made no mention of a power to sell or mortgage trust assets. Under these circumstances:

(A) Edward violated his fiduciary duty by selling the trust asset.

(B) Edward violated his fiduciary duty in purchasing the trust asset for himself, regardless of whether he paid the fair market value of the property.

(C) Edward violated his fiduciary duty in purchasing the trust asset for himself, but only if he paid less than the fair market value for this asset.

(D) Edward did not violate his fiduciary duty.

77. Suppose that, in Question 76, Edward had, in his capacity as trustee, elected to borrow funds, using the office building as security for the debt, and had then invested the borrowed funds in higher income-yielding assets. Under these circumstances:

(A) Edward breached his fiduciary duty.

(B) Edward breached his fiduciary duty, if the net income of the trust is reduced by his actions.

(C) Edward breached his fiduciary duty by borrowing funds, if he has the power to sell the asset.

(D) Edward did not breach his fiduciary duty.

78. Claire created a testamentary trust as follows:

> The trustee shall pay so much of the income as she shall, in her sole, absolute and uncontrolled discretion, determine is necessary for the care, maintenance and support of my children, until my youngest child shall reach the age of 25 years, at which time all accrued income and principal shall be distributed to my children, share and share alike.

At Claire's death all of her three children were minors. The trustee thereafter paid all of the income annually to the oldest child. When the youngest child reached the age of 25, the two youngest children sued the trustee, claiming that the trustee had breached her fiduciary duty by not previously paying any of the income to them. Under these circumstances:

(A) The court has no power to review the "sole, absolute and uncontrolled" discretionary decisions of the trustee.

(B) Although the court has the power to review discretionary decisions of the trustee, the trustee will be presumed to have acted reasonably under these circumstances.

(C) The court has the power to review the discretionary decisions of the trustee, and to impose liability for those decisions made arbitrarily or in bad faith.

(D) The court has the power to review the discretionary decisions of the trustee, and to impose liability for those decisions which the court believes were not sound.

79. Ted is the trustee of an *inter vivos* trust. The trust res is comprised of $300,000 in cash. The beneficiaries are Ted's nephews and nieces. Ted recently located a parcel of unimproved property that is available for sale. The price of the property is $300,000, and Ted projects that the property will increase in value to $500,000 within two years. Under these circumstances, Ted may:

(A) Invest in this property, if a prudent investor would do so.

(B) Invest in this property, if he obtains an appraisal showing that the value of the property is now at least $300,000.

(C) Not invest in this property, regardless of what the trust instrument authorizes.

(D) Not invest in this property, unless the trust instrument specifically authorizes real estate investments.

80. Able and Baker were appointed co-trustees of a trust created by Mabel Schultz. In the course of administering the trust, they initiated a lawsuit against a real estate agent who they felt had defrauded the trust. The case was tried and judgment was rendered in favor of the real estate agent. Both Able and the trust's attorney believe the case was wrongly decided. Able wishes to appeal the judgment but Baker refuses to do so. Under these circumstances:

(A) Able may appeal the judgment unilaterally; but if the appeal is unsuccessful, Able is personally responsible for all costs of appeal.

(B) Able may appeal the judgment without Baker's consent.

(C) Able may not appeal the judgment without Baker's consent.

(D) Baker may not refuse to join in the appeal, since to do so would be a breach of his fiduciary duties.

81. Karl, a college professor, is the trustee of a trust created by his father-in-law for the benefit of Karl's children. Karl accepted a visiting professorship at Cambridge University for an academic year. Because he was going to be out of the country, Karl retained Edward, a stockbroker, to act as the substitute trustee for that year. Karl executed a document authorizing Edward to "exercise all powers and fulfill all duties which I now possess as trustee." Under these circumstances:

(A) Karl is effectively relieved of his duties as trustee during the year, and is not liable for any breach of fiduciary duties which might occur.

(B) Karl is not relieved of liability for any breach of fiduciary duties, but properly delegated the powers of the trustee to Edward.

(C) Karl is not relieved of liability for any breach of fiduciary duties, but Edward may exercise all discretionary powers of the trustee under the trust.

(D) Karl has breached his fiduciary duty and is liable for all damages resulting from Edward's acts or omissions.

82. Suppose that, in Question 81, Edward was employed by Karl to make investment decisions pertaining to trust assets. Karl unquestioningly adhered to Edward's suggestions, which were based upon Edward's judgment alone. One of the securities purchased for the trust at Edward's suggestion dropped in value, causing a significant loss to the trust estate. Under these circumstances:

(A) Karl is liable to the trust, if (and only if) a prudent investor would not have purchased the stock.

(B) Karl is liable to the trust, without regard to whether a prudent investor would have purchased the stock.

(C) Karl is liable to the trust, only if Edward failed to act as a competent stockbroker.

(D) To determine if Karl is liable to the trust it is necessary to determine if he utilized reasonable care in selecting Edward to make investment decisions.

83. Suppose that, in Question 81, Karl loaned trust funds to himself at a higher rate of interest than the prevailing market rate for similar loans. Karl used the loan to invest in several new stocks, which he later sold at a substantial profit. Upon selling the stocks, Karl repaid the loans to the trust, together with all accrued interest. Under these circumstances, Karl:

(A) Breached his fiduciary duty to the trust, but no damage has occurred.

(B) Breached his fiduciary duty to the trust, and must remit the profits which he made on the sale of the stock to the trust.

(C) Has not breached his fiduciary duty to the trust, but would have been liable for any losses which the trust might have suffered in this type of transaction.

(D) Has not breached any duty to the trust, since he had promised to pay and did pay a higher rate of interest than the market rate.

84. Amy is the trustee of a testamentary trust which consists of $300,000 in cash. The trust instrument provides that Amy is entitled to receive trust income which is "necessary to her proper support, maintenance and education." The principal passes to Amy's children upon her death. Amy recently purchased a business for the trust for $100,000. However, because she failed to research the new business carefully, she subsequently learned that there were several lawsuits pending against it. As a consequence, the business was actually worth only $25,000. The trust document has a provision which states: "The trustee shall not be liable for negligence in administering the trust assets, or any activity undertaken on behalf of the trust." Under these circumstances:

(A) Amy would not be liable for any losses which occurred, under any circumstances.

(B) Amy is liable for the loss incurred by the trust corpus, but not for any loss of income.

(C) Amy is liable for the loss of trust income, but not the loss of corpus.

(D) Amy would not be liable for the losses, unless her actions amounted to gross negligence.

85. Laura is the trustee of an *inter vivos* trust, the ABC Trust. She signed a contract with Xavier whereby Xavier was to perform certain accounting services for the trust. (Laura signed the contract, "Laura, as trustee for the ABC Trust.") A *bona fide* dispute arose concerning whether Xavier had adequately performed the services. Laura refused to pay (or have the trust pay) for the services. Xavier sued Laura personally on the contract. If Xavier prevails on the merits:

(A) Laura will be personally liable for breach of contract, but may indemnify herself from trust assets (assuming she acted in good faith).

(B) Laura will not be personally liable for breach of contract, because she may be sued only in her capacity as trustee.

(C) Laura will be personally liable for breach of contract, and may not be indemnified from trust assets.

(D) Laura will be personally liable for breach of contract, and may not be indemnified from trust assets unless the trust instrument specifically contains an exculpatory clause.

86. Bill, the trustee of an *inter vivos* trust having a trust res of $500,000, negligently struck Phyllis while driving his car. At the time, he was on his way to a meeting with the trust's investment adviser. Phyllis sued Bill, individually and as trustee of the trust, for her damages ($300,000). Under these circumstances:

(A) Bill is personally liable for any judgment, but may indemnify himself from the trust's assets.

(B) Bill is not personally liable for any judgment, but may be sued in his capacity as trustee of the trust.

(C) Bill is personally liable for any judgment, and may *not* be indemnified from trust assets.

(D) Bill is personally liable for any judgment, and may not be indemnified from trust assets, unless the trust instrument specifically contains an exculpatory clause.

87. Suppose that, in Question 86, (1) the tort was committed by an employee of the trust who was hired by Bill, while on trust business, and (2) the damages sustained by Phyllis were $600,000. Under these circumstances:

(A) Bill is personally liable for the damages, but may seek indemnity from the trust and, to the extent not satisfied therefrom, may seek indemnity from the beneficiaries.

(B) Bill is personally liable for the damages, and may seek indemnity from the trust, but only to the extent of the trust assets.

(C) Bill is not personally liable for the damages, but must pay such damages from the trust assets.

(D) Neither Bill nor the trust assets are liable for the woman's damages, but she can recover from Bill's employee.

88. Ben created a testamentary trust by bequeathing 300 shares of Bloomfield, Inc. common stock to Adams National Bank, as trustee. The trustee was instructed to pay the income to Ben's children for life, and the remainder to his grandchildren at the death of the last survivor of his children. Bloomfield has a net profit for the current year. However, due to plans to expand its facilities, it does not wish to declare cash dividends. It has decided to declare a stock dividend of one share for each four shares of stock currently owned by shareholders. The trust created by Ben will receive 75 shares of Bloomfield, Inc. common stock. Under these circumstances, the trustee should:

(A) Add the stock dividend shares to the corpus of the trust.

(B) Distribute the stock dividend shares to the income beneficiaries.

(C) Distribute half of the stock dividend to the income beneficiaries, and the other half to the corpus of the trust.

(D) Distribute stock equal in value to the cash dividend which would have been declared but for the expansion plans to the income beneficiaries, and add the remainder of the stock to the trust corpus.

89. Taft Trust company is the trustee of a trust created by Marlon Cando. Marlon transferred certain real estate to the trust with instructions to use the income therefrom "for the relief of the poverty of American Indians." After 20 years, the trust corpus is to be paid to the Animal Welfare League. Taft has determined that, of the three properties conveyed to it as trustee, two are unproductive, in that they produce no current income. Under these circumstances:

(A) Taft is not obligated to sell the two properties; but if it does so, all proceeds are allocated to the corpus of the trust.

(B) Taft is not obligated to sell the properties; but if it does so, the original fair market value of the properties at the time the trust was created must be allocated to corpus and any appreciation in value allocated to income.

(C) Taft is obligated to sell the two properties, and all proceeds must be allocated to corpus.

(D) Taft is obligated to sell the two properties; and the original fair market value of the properties at the time the trust was created must be allocated to corpus, and any appreciation allocated to income.

90. Louise is the trustee of a trust created by her mother. The income beneficiaries of the trust are Louise and her two brothers. The remaindermen are Louise's two sisters. The corpus of the trust consists of two income-producing properties. During the course of each year, the trust must pay for maintenance, real estate taxes and insurance on the properties. Under these circumstances:

(A) Maintenance is charged to the income beneficiaries; but taxes and insurance are chargeable against the corpus of the trust.

(B) Maintenance and taxes are charged to the income beneficiaries; but insurance is chargeable against the corpus of the trust.

(C) Taxes and insurance are chargeable against the income beneficiaries; but maintenance is chargeable against the corpus of the trust.

(D) Maintenance, taxes and insurance are chargeable to the income beneficiaries, exclusively.

91. Ellen created an *inter vivos* trust by transferring $100,000 in trust to First National Bank, as trustee, for the benefit of her children for life, with the remainder to her grandchildren. The trust document did not state whether Ellen retained the power to revoke or modify the trust. After the creation of the trust, Ellen delivered a letter to the trustee, advising it that she wished to revoke the remainder gift to the grandchildren and to substitute her nephews as remaindermen. The trustee rejected Ellen's modification of the trust. Angered by the trustee's response, Ellen delivered a second letter to the trustee, revoking the trust in its entirety. The trustee rejected this letter also. Under these circumstances, Ellen is entitled to:

(A) Modify the trust by revoking the gift to the remaindermen and substituting her nephews, but cannot revoke the trust in its entirety.

(B) Revoke the trust in its entirety, but cannot modify it.

(C) Modify and revoke the trust.

(D) Neither revoke nor modify the trust.

Multiple-Choice Answers

1. **D** When a decedent dies ***intestate***, survived by a spouse and surviving descendants who are also descendants of the surviving spouse and there is no other descendant of the surviving spouse who survives the decedent, the surviving spouse takes the entire estate (UPC § 2-102(1)(ii)). Since Rosa is survived by her husband Bill and two children who are descendants of Rosa as well as of Bill, Bill takes the entire estate. Choices **A**, **B**, and **C** are all incorrect under the rules for intestacy contained in the UPC.

2. **C** An heir who does not survive the decedent by ***120 hours*** is deemed to have predeceased the decedent (UPC § 2-104). Since Wanda is deemed to have predeceased Jim, her estate takes nothing. The deceased daughter's grandchildren are entitled to take their parent's share of the estate by right of representation. UPC § 2-103(1). Thus, the estate is split into two shares of $100,000 each. Bob takes one share and the grandchildren split the other share. Choices **A** and **B** are incorrect, because they assume that Wanda is entitled to take a share of the estate. Choice **D** is incorrect, because it assumes that Bob and the grandchildren take *per capita* instead of by representation.

3. **B** If after executing a will, the testator is ***divorced***, the divorce ***revokes any testamentary disposition*** to the former spouse, unless the will provides otherwise (UPC § 2-804(b)). Because Leonard and Evelyn were divorced, her gift was revoked (even though she survived him). The gift over to Leonard's mother and father fails because they did not survive him. Leonard's sister and brother take in place of Leonard's parents pursuant to the anti-lapse statute, because they are descendants of a beneficiary related to the testator (UPC § 2-603(b)). Although Sue was a witness to the will, the will is valid and the gift to her is also valid so long as there is no showing of undue influence by her. UPC § 2-505. Choice **A** is incorrect because it presumes the gift to Evelyn was not revoked by the divorce. Choice **C** is incorrect because it assumes Sue cannot take because she was an interested witness. Choice **D** is incorrect; there is no basis for precluding Ted from inheriting.

4. **B** This is an unusually tricky question, so follow closely. Any person 18 or older who is of sound mind may make a will. Every non-holographic will must be in writing signed by the testator and by two other persons each of whom witnessed either the signing or the testator's acknowledgment of either (a) the signature or (b) that the document is a will. A mark made by the testator suffices as a signature. The will was valid because Dan was 19, he signed the document with a mark, and the execution of the will was witnessed by two witnesses. Because Dan's mother predeceased him, the gift to her fails.

Under the anti-lapse statute, Les would normally take his mother's share, as her sole descendant — but this would happen as a "substitute gift," not by having Dan's property pass through the mother's estate. (UPC § 2-603). However, § 2-601 says that the anti-lapse provision applies "only in the absence of a finding of a contrary intention. . .." A court would probably conclude that the language in the will disinheriting Les manifests Dan's intent not to have the anti-lapse provision apply. If so, the estate would pass by intestacy since all bequests would have failed. Here, too, Les would ordinarily take, under § 2-103(3). But again, the UPC honors the testator's wishes: § 2-101(b) protects a decedent's choice to "expressly exclude or limit the right of an individual. . . to succeed to property of the decedent passing by intestate succession." The disinheritance language here would certainly meet this test. Consequently, the estate would go to the next in line -- the decedent's grandmother. UPC § 2-103(4). Choice **A** is incorrect, since Dan's mother predeceased him. Choices **C** and **D** are incorrect. Les takes nothing for the reasons described above.

5.   **A**   An adopted child is treated as a natural born child for purposes of inheritance. (UPC § 2-114(b)). Lisa will inherit equally with Tom because she was adopted by Ellen. The $10,000 will not be treated as an advancement, since the only evidence of Ellen's intent was oral. (§ 2-109(a) requires that if an individual dies intestate, advancements must be established as such either in a writing contemporaneous with the gift signed by the testator or in a written acknowledgment by the heir.) Because the condition upon Tom's gift was oral and not written, Lisa and Tom will each take $75,000. Choice **B** is incorrect because it assumes that the $10,000 will be treated as an advancement against Tom's share of the estate. Choice **C** is incorrect because it assumes that Lisa is not treated as Ellen's child for purposes of inheritance. Choice **D** is incorrect because it fails to provide for inheritance by Tom.

6.   **C**   A spouse who married the testator after the making of the testator's will takes an intestate share unless: (1) it appears from the will or other evidence that the will was made in contemplation of the testator's marriage to the surviving spouse; (2) the will expresses the intention that its terms should be effective notwithstanding any subsequent marriage; or (3) the testator provided for the spouse by transfer outside the will, and the intent that the transfer be in lieu of a testamentary provision is shown by the testator's statements or can be reasonably inferred from the amount

of the transfer or other evidence (UPC § 2-301). None of these conditions appears to be satisfied here; therefore, Edward takes an intestate share. If no descendant of the decedent survives the decedent, but a parent of the decedent survives the decedent, the spouse's intestate share is the first $200,000, plus three-fourths of any balance of the intestate estate. UPC § 2-102(2). So Edward gets this amount, with the remaining one-fourth going to the Laura's mother. Choice **A** is incorrect in that it does not provide for Edward at all. Choice **B** is incorrect in that it does not provide for Laura's mother. Choice **D** is incorrect in that it misstates the respective shares of Edward and Laura's mother.

7. **A**   A writing which is in existence when a will is executed may be ***incorporated by reference***, if the language of the will manifests the intent to incorporate and describes the writing sufficiently to permit its identification (UPC § 2-510). In this case, the will relies upon an extrinsic document (John's *inter vivos* trust) to identify the devisees. The trust was executed prior to Ann's will and is described sufficiently to allow incorporation. Since Adrian and Kimberly were the only income beneficiaries at the time of Ann's death, they take equally. Choice **B** is incorrect because (contrary to the facts) it indicates that Ann intended to put the bequest in trust. The trust was incorporated merely to identify the beneficiaries under Ann's will. The devisees are given Ann's estate free of trust. Choices **C** and **D** are incorrect. Rita, John and Lisa do not take any part of the $100,000 bequest.

8. **B**   A will may dispose of property by ***reference to acts and events which have significance apart from their effect upon dispositions made by the testator*** in his will (whether they occur before or after the execution of the will, or before or after the testator's death). The execution or revocation of a will of another person is such an event (UPC § 2-512). The will of Bill's mother is an event of independent significance because the statute expressly provides for the execution or revocation of another individual's will. Because State University was the residuary legatee in the will of Bill's mother, it will get the $500,000 bequest. Choice **A** is incorrect because Bill's mother revoked the will under which Tim and Tom would take. Choice **C** would be correct only if the gift to State University had failed. Choice **D** is incorrect. If the gift to State University had failed, the money would have passed under the residuary clause to the American Red Cross.

9. **A**   A specific devisee has the right to ***any balance*** of the purchase price owing from a purchaser by reason of the testator's sale of the property, together with any security agreement by the purchaser. (UPC § 2-

606(a)(1)). The devise of the condominium was specific; it can be identified as against all other assets of the testator's estate. Although a gift of specifically devised property is ordinarily adeemed when the property is sold during the testator's lifetime, the balance due and owing to the decedent from the buyer is not adeemed. Choices **B**, **C** and **D** are incorrect becausenon-ademption occurs only with respect to the ***unpaid*** purchase price; the gift is adeemed to the extent of the pre-death sales proceeds (*i.e.*, the funds in the bank account), unless the surrounding circumstances indicate that the testator would not have wanted ademption to occur, which is not the case here. UPC § 2-606(a)(6).

10. C   A devisee of ***stocks*** is entitled to (1) any additional or other securities of the same entity owned by the testator at death by reason of action (such as a stock split or stock dividend) initiated by that entity, and (2) any securities ***of another entity*** owned by the testator as a result of a merger, consolidation, reorganization, or other similar action *(*UPC § 2-605). When ABC split its stock and declared a stock dividend (actions initiated by ABC), the additional shares became part of the bequest of stock to Edna. When XYZ made a tender offer, the shares of XYZ stock received by Kathy took the place of the ABC shares. The final 40 shares of XYZ stock were purchased subsequently by Kathy, and so were not part of the original bequest of ABC stock. Choice **A** is incorrect because the 40 shares of XYZ subsequently purchased by Kathy are not included in the devise to Edna. Choice **B** is incorrect because the shares resulting from the stock split and stock dividend, as well as the XYZ shares received in the merger, pass to Edna. Choice **D** is incorrect. Even if none of the XYZ shares were to pass to Edna, they would be distributed to Kay under the terms of Kathy's will, not to Bill.

11. B   Larry did not own the second home when the will was executed, and his later purchase of it was not an act that met testamentary formalities; however, the purchase was an act that had significance apart from its effect on the will (*i.e.*, Larry bought it because he wanted to live in it). Under the "acts of independent significance" doctrine, the will would be interpreted to mean "the home I own at my death." Larry's home will be distributed to Ron, as specified in the will. *See* UPC § 2-512.

The issue then becomes whether the conveyance of the first home to Ron, and/or the cash gift to Carolyn, acted as a full or partial satisfaction of the specific bequests to them. A lifetime gift of property to a devisee is treated as a satisfaction only if: (1) the will provides for deduction of the gift; (2) the testator declares in a contemporaneous writing that the gifts are in satisfaction of the devise or that their value is to be deducted from the value of the devise; or (3) the devisees acknowledge in writing that the gifts are in satisfaction of the devise or that their value is to be deducted from the value of the devise. (UPC § 2-609). None of these conditions was satisfied as to either the house-transfer to Ron or the cash gift to Carolyn. Larry's estate will therefore be distributed according to the terms of his will. Choice **A** is incorrect because it assumes satisfaction of both gifts. Choice **C** is incorrect because it assumes satisfaction of the gift to Ron. Choice **D** is incorrect because it fails to distribute all of the cash to Carolyn.

12. **D**   A person who kills another intentionally and feloniously loses any right to benefit financially from her victim's estate, whether the assets are part of the probate estate or pass outside the estate. This principle is codified in § 2-803(c)(1), which provides that the felonious and intentional killing of the decedent "revokes any revocable . . . disposition . . . of property made by the decedent to the killer in a governing instrument. . . ." Both wills and insurance policies are covered in the definition of "governing instrument" (§ 1-201(19)). The bequest to Sofia and the designation of her as policy beneficiary, are both cancelled. Therefore, the cash and insurance proceeds pass into Bert's intestate estate.

Under UPC § 2-803(c)(2), the felonious and intentional killing also "severs the interests of the decedent and killer in property held by them at the time of the killing as joint tenants with the right of survivorship, transforming the interests of the decedent and killer into tenancies in common." Therefore, Bert's intestate estate holds a 1/2 interest in the home as tenant in common; this tenancy then passes to the grandchildren equally. Choice **A** is incorrect in that it assumes the conviction of murder has no effect upon any of the assets owned by Bert. Choice **B** is incorrect in that it assumes that the conviction affects distribution of probate assets only, not the insurance policy or the joint tenancy in the home. Choice **C** is incorrect in that it also assumes the conviction does not affect an insurance policy.

13. **A**   When a second will — which revoked the first will — is thereafter revoked by physical act, the first will is *revived* if it is evident from (1) the *circumstances* under which the second will is revoked, or (2) the testator's contemporary or subsequent *declarations,* that he *intended the first will to take effect* as executed. (UPC § 2-509(a)). Although the second will expressly revoked the first will, the statements of Jamir that his father should take the estate under the first will evidenced an intent to revive the first after destruction of the second will. Choice **B** is incorrect because the second will was revoked by physical act. Choice **C** is incor-

rect because the first will was revived and is in effect. Choice **D** is incorrect for a new reason--Jamir's mother and father, not his sisters, would take by intestate succession if the first will were not revived.

14. **C**   As in Question 13, the tearing up of the second will was a "revocatory act" that revoked that will. UPC § 2-507(a)(2). Under these new facts, there are no direct statements by Jamir supporting revival of the first instrument. On the contrary, we have Jamir's statement deriding all wills. That being so, the first will remains revoked by the second will. Therefore, Jamir's estate passes by intestate succession (*i.e.*, to his mother and father equally). Choices **A** and **B** are incorrect because neither will survives and Jamir died intestate. Choice **D** is incorrect because Jamir's father and mother (rather than his sisters) would take by intestate succession.

15. **D**   A will is **revoked** by a subsequent will which is **inconsistent** with the former instrument (UPC § 2-507). Will #2 revoked Will #1 by inconsistency. Since Will #3 revoked Will #2, but gives no indication that revival of the first will was intended, revival of Will #1 will *not* occur. See UPC § 2-509(c). Thus, Edgar died intestate and his estate should be divided between Tom and Wilma. Choice **A** is incorrect because Will #3 indicates no intention by Edgar to reinstate Will #1. Choice **B** is incorrect because Will #2 was expressly revoked by Will #3. Choice **C** is incorrect because the facts stipulate that Will #3 was revoked by physical act.

16. **A**   A will, including a holographic will, may refer to a written statement or list to dispose of tangible personal property not otherwise specifically disposed of by the will. To be admissible, the writing must (1) be either in the testator's handwriting or signed by her, and (2) describe the items and the devisees with reasonable certainty (UPC § 2-513). Even though the list could *not* be incorporated by reference (*i.e.*, it was created after the will) and has no significance apart from its testamentary effect, inclusion of the list is permitted under this rule. Choice **B** is incorrect because the bequest is effective as written and the items do not fall into the residue. Choice **C** is incorrect; there is no indication that this property was specifically devised to Rusty and Rosa. Choice **D** is incorrect because if the bequests listed in the writing failed, they would pass as part of the residuary gift, not in intestacy.

17. **B**   Since Roberta was not survived by issue, her gifts (the piano and her residuary share) lapse and pass through the residuary clause. Where a gift (residuary or other) is given to a class comprised of lineal descendants from the decedent's grandparents, the descendants of a prede-

ceased class member take that member's share (UPC § 2-603); therefore, Ted's son takes Ted's share of the residue, along with Edwina and Judy. Choice **A** is incorrect because Roberta's gifts lapsed and no one can take through her. (Roberta died without descendants). Choice **C** is incorrect because Ted's child is entitled to share in the residue as Ted's descendant. Choice **D** is incorrect in that the anti-lapse statute provides only for **descendants** of a predeceased member of the designated class, not a **spouse**.

18. D   A person who is a devisee under a testamentary instrument may **disclaim** the right of succession to any property or interest therein by filing a **written** disclaimer (UPC § 2-801(a)). Because Albert renounced his gift, he is treated as though he had predeceased the testator. If Albert had predeceased Tim, the anti-lapse statute would have come into play: because Albert is a descendant of a grandparent of the testator and was himself survived by a descendant, that descendant (Albert's son) would take the real estate under the anti-lapse statute. Consequently, Albert's disclaimer means that his son takes the real estate. The remainder of the estate is divided among Tim's brothers and sister. Choice **A** is incorrect because a devisee is expressly permitted to disclaim his interest in a devise. Choice **B** is incorrect because the anti-lapse statute applies when a devisee is deemed to have predeceased the testator. Choice **C** is incorrect in that the gift of the real estate would become part of the residue if it were deemed to fail and would go to Tim's brothers and sister, not to the children he had disinherited.

19. A   A specific devise passes the property, subject to any mortgage interest existing at the date of death, without right of exoneration (regardless of a general directive in the will to pay debts). (UPC § 2-607). Even though this may result in an unequal distribution of assets on these facts, there is no specific directive by Tom to pay the debt secured by the mortgage from the general assets of the estate. Choice **B** is incorrect because there is no specific directive by Tom to pay the debt secured by the mortgage. Choice **C** is incorrect because there is no provision for a gift of stock to Joan in the will. Choice **D** is incorrect. The court must distribute Tom's estate in accordance with terms of the will, not according to its conjectures about Tom's possible motives.

20. A   Since paternity was established prior to John's death, Jennifer is treated as his child (UPC § 2-114(a)). Jennifer is a pretermitted child (Jennifer was born after John had made his will). A pretermitted child (the UPC refers to an "omitted" child) takes as if her parent had died intestate. (UPC § 2-302). When testator is unmarried and leaves only one child, that child's intestate share is the entire estate. (UPC § 2-103(1)). There-fore, Jennifer receives the entire estate. Choice **B** is incorrect because Jennifer's claim to the intestate share as a pretermitted child supersedes the devise to ABC. Choices **C** and **D** are incorrect because they do not state Jennifer's share correctly--Jennifer is entitled to the entire estate.

21. **B**   Normally, when a decedent dies intestate without a spouse or descen-dants, the estate is split between the decedent's parents, if both survive. UPC § 2-103(2). However, the fact that paternity is established against a father is ineffective to qualify him or his heirs to inherit from or through the child born out of wedlock, unless the father has (1) openly treated the child as his, **and** (2) has not refused to support the child (UPC § 2-114(c)). Although John supported Jennifer, he refused to treat her as his own child. Thus, he is disqualified from inheriting from or through her. Because Jennifer has no surviving spouse and no issue, Betty, as Jenni-fer's only parent entitled to inherit from her, inherits Jennifer's entire estate. Choice **A** is incorrect because John is *not* qualified to inherit. Choices **C** and **D** are incorrect because Betty takes Jennifer's entire estate under the principles governing intestacy (UPC § 2-103(2)).

22. **B**   Relatives of the half-blood inherit the same as if they were of the whole-blood (UPC § 2-107). Although Kane is a half-brother of Mark (*i.e.*, they share only one common parent), he is entitled to inherit from Mark just as if he were a whole-blood brother. Mark died without surviving issue or parents. (Steve is not Mark's "parent," because that term "excludes any person who is only a stepparent. . ." UPC § 1-201(33)). Therefore, Will and Kane as Mark's brothers share Mark's estate equally. (UPC § 2-103(3).) Choice **A** is incorrect since Kane is entitled to inherit equally with Will. Choices **C** and **D** are incorrect because Steve is not related to Mark in the degree required by the principles gov-erning intestacy.

23. **B**   An heir of the decedent conceived before his death, but born thereafter, *inherits in the same way as if born in the decedent's lifetime* (UPC § 2-108). Because Ted left descendants and a surviving spouse *and* the sur-viving spouse has one or more surviving descendants who are not descendants of the decedent, Judy, as surviving spouse, takes the first $150,000 plus one-half of the balance of the estate (UPC § 2-102(3)). Because Ted, Jr. was conceived prior to Ted's death and was born after Ted's death, he shares the remaining one-half with his sister Lisa (UPC § 2-103(1)). Choice **A** is incorrect in that it excludes Ted, Jr. from his

inheritance. Choice **C** is incorrect in that it misstates Judy's share. Choice **D** is incorrect in that it misstates Judy's share and excludes Ted, Jr. from any inheritance.

24. A The facts here differ in that two of Ted's descendants were not also descendants of his wife Judy. If there are surviving descendants of the decedent, one or more of whom are *not* descendants of the surviving spouse, the intestate share of the surviving spouse is $100,000, plus one-half of the balance of the estate. (UPC § 2-102(4)). Since Ted left descendants, at least one of whom is not a descendant of Judy, Judy's intestate share is $100,000, plus one-half of the balance of the estate. Because Ted Jr., was conceived prior to the death of Ted and was born after Ted's death, he is treated as having survived Ted, and he therefore takes one-third of the remainder, along with Lisa and Amy. Choice **B** is incorrect in that it excludes Ted, Jr. from any inheritance. Choice **C** is incorrect in that it misstates Judy's share. Choice **D** is incorrect in that it misstates Judy's share and excludes Ted, Jr. from any inheritance.

25. B Foster children do not ordinarily inherit from their foster parents. UPC § 1-201(5) defines "child" so as to exclude "a foster child." However, most jurisdictions recognize "adoption by estoppel" when there is an unperformed agreement to adopt. In this case, the statement made to Lisa could reasonably have been interpreted by her as a promise of adoption. Taken together with the fact that Harvey and Ann "held Lisa out as their daughter," most jurisdictions would probably treat Lisa as an adopted child by estopping Harvey's estate from denying that an adoption existed. If there are surviving descendants of the decedent, one or more of whom are not descendants of the surviving spouse, the intestate share of the surviving spouse is $100,000, plus one-half of the balance of the estate. (UPC § 2-102(4)). Since Harvey left a descendant, Bob, who is not a descendant of Ann, Ann's intestate share is $100,000, plus one-half of the remainder along with Bob. Choice **A** is incorrect because it would control the distribution only if Harvey had no descendants. Choice **C** is incorrect in that it misstates Ann's share. Choice **D** is incorrect. It applies only if all of the decedent's surviving descendants were also descendants of the surviving spouse. Here, Harvey had a son by a previous marriage.

26. C In most jurisdictions, a testator's explanation of her motives in making a testamentary document will not ordinarily be interpreted as a condition to the effectiveness of the document. *In re Taylor's Estate*, 119 Cal.

App. 2d, 574(1953); *Eaton v. Brown,* 193 U.S. 411 (1904). The inference here would be that Patricia was prompted to make her will at this time because she was about to make the trip, not that she wished her will to be ignored if she returned. The writing is a valid holographic will. Choice **A** is incorrect because there is no requirement in the UPC that a holographic will be dated to be enforceable. Choice **B** is incorrect because the will is effective, and, in any event, if the will were not effective, Patricia's mother would inherit the entire estate (UPC § 2-103(2)). Choice **D** is incorrect. There is no interpretation under which the two would share. Either the Art Museum would take (if the will is valid) or the mother would take (if the will is not valid), but *not* both.

27. A   A contract to make a will or testamentary gift, or not to revoke a will or testamentary gift, can be established only by: (1) provisions of a will stating material provisions of the contract; (2) an express reference in the will to an agreement and extrinsic evidence proving the terms of that contract; or (3) a writing signed by the decedent evidencing the contract (UPC § 2-514). (Note that this section does not preclude one from recovering in *quantum meruit* for the value of services rendered.) Because the agreement here is not evidenced in writing (either in Clay's will or in a separate document signed by Clay), it cannot be enforced by Arnold against Clay's estate. Therefore, Anne will take under the will. Choice **B** is incorrect because the agreement with Arnold was oral and not referred to in Clay's will; therefore, it cannot be proved. Choice **C** is incorrect. Even if the agreement could be proved, Arnold would take to the exclusion of Tom. Choice **D** is incorrect. The will, which is effective, leaves Clay's entire estate to Anne.

28. D   A contract to make a testamentary gift is generally not enforceable during the testator's lifetime. If the testator, however, either orally or by his actions, repudiates the contract after the promisee has substantially performed or acted in reliance on the contract, the promisee may ordinarily sue for anticipatory breach and seek to impose a constructive trust upon the assets in the hands of a third party. Because Clay has transferred a substantial portion of his assets after promising to leave his entire estate to Arnold, his conduct will probably be viewed as an anticipatory breach. Arnold may sue to have a constructive trust imposed on the assets transferred by Clay to Tom. Tom would probably *not* be deprived of their use during Clay's lifetime, but would be ordered to transfer the assets to Arnold at Clay's death (pursuant to Clay's agreement with Arnold). Choice **A** is incorrect because Arnold has no right to possession of the assets until Clay's death. Choice **B** is incorrect. The assessment of damages before Clay's death would be speculative and difficult. Arnold might die before Clay. Choice **C** is incorrect because Arnold has no right to control Clay's assets until Clay's death.

29. A   A will, the original of which cannot be produced in court, can nevertheless be proved. UPC § 3-402(a). However, the burden is ordinarily on the proponents of the will to prove that the will was duly executed. UPC § 3-407. Because Toni's attorney can testify as to the execution of the will and her conversation with Toni shortly before Toni's death, this burden is probably carried. Choices **B** and **D** are incorrect because neither choice correctly allocates Toni's estate, even if the will is not probated (*i.e.*, Rob and Adam would divide the estate equally) (UPC § 2-103(1)). Choice **C** would be the correct answer *if* the will were not admitted to probate.

30. B   Where there are no members of a class in existence when a will is executed or at the testator's death, members of the class (whenever born) ordinarily receive their gifts when the class can be determined. We can assume that Parker knew that his best friend had no children and that he wanted the distribution to Sam's children postponed until all of the class members could be determined. Choice **A** is incorrect in that it does not include all of Sam's children. Choice **C** is incorrect because Parker did not provide for Ann and was not required to provide for her. Choice **D** is incorrect because Parker's estate would pass to his parents only if the will was invalid (UPC § 2-103(2)).

31. A   When a will makes a gift to a class, it is presumed that the testator would want the class to close at his death, provided any members of the class are alive. This is sometimes called the *"Rule of Convenience."* Because Bob was the only member of the class alive at the time of Parker's death, he would take the entire estate. Choice **B** is incorrect. Under the Rule of Convenience, the class closed at Parker's death (after-born class members do not participate). Choice **C** is incorrect because Parker was not required to provide for Ann . Choice **D** is incorrect because Parker's estate would pass to his parents only if the will was invalid (UPC § 2-103(2)) .

32. B   Under the Rule of Convenience, the class closes when the first member of the class is entitled to distribution. The class would close when Bob reached age 25; only Bob and Ellen were alive when Bob reached 25. Bob's and Ellen's shares would be retained until each reached 25, and would be distributed to him or her as he or she reached that age. If either died before reaching age 25, his or her share would be distributed to the survivor of them. Choice **A** is incorrect because Ellen is a prospective member of the class. Choice **C** is incorrect because Sally was born after the class closed (when Bob reached 25) and therefore is not a member of the class. Choice **D** is incorrect since Bob and Ellen must reach age 25 before he or she takes, and Sally is not a member of the class.

33. C When a testator makes specific *per capita* bequests to members of a class and there are no members of the class living at testator's death, the gift fails. The bequests fail because the amount of each bequest does not vary and the total cannot be determined. Because there were no takers at Parker's death, the gift fails altogether. When no residuary clause is expressed in the will, property not disposed of by the will passes by intestate succession. Here, the entire estate passes by intestacy. Choices **A** and **B** are incorrect because Bob, Sally and Ellen were not alive at Parker's death and Ann would not inherit by intestacy. Choice **D** is incorrect because Parker's parents would inherit under the rules governing intestacy principles.

34. D The mere execution of joint wills or reciprocal wills does not create the presumption of a contract by either testator not to revoke his or her will. There is no evidence of a contract between Edward and Mary not to revoke the original wills. Edward was therefore free to execute a new will. Answer **A** is incorrect in that Edward's first will was revoked by the inconsistent disposition made in his second will. Answer **B** is incorrect in that the second will is valid and that Edward did not die intestate. Answer **C** is incorrect. If Edward had died intestate, one-half of his estate would pass to his grandchildren, the issue of his predeceased daughter Lisa.

35. D In most states, only "interested parties" may contest a will. An interested party is one who is **adversely affected** by the will's admission to probate. If the second will here is probated, Jim gets $10,000 more than he would have received under the prior will. Because he is not adversely affected, he cannot contest. Only Elizabeth has standing, since she takes everything under the first will, but suffers a $10,000 reduction under the second will. Answers **A** and **B** are incorrect because Jim's interest is not adversely affected under the second will (*i.e.*, he gets more than he would have if the first will remained in effect). Answer **C** is incorrect, since neither Jim nor either of Bill's parents is adversely affected by the second will. Bill's parents take nothing under either will, and the first will is conceded to be valid.

36. A When a will provision is the product of an insane delusion of the testator, that provision will not be given effect by the probate court. An insane delusion is sometimes described as "a belief that is the product of the imagination and is held tenaciously against all evidence and reason to the contrary." Haskell, p. 42. John's belief about Clay's illegitimacy would seem to qualify: there is no evidence that Clay was conceived as the consequence of an illicit relationship; in fact, the evidence (the blood typing) is to the contrary. The will establishes that John was driven to make his will disinheriting Clay by his irrational belief. On the other hand, there is no evidence that John was otherwise irrational or incompetent to make a will. The court will attempt to admit the will to probate without enforcing the clause relating to Clay. However, because excision of the clause will not remedy the wrong to Clay (Clay still won't get anything), the court will probably refuse to admit the whole will to probate on these facts. This will produce a more just result (Clay takes in intestacy). Answer **B** is incorrect. Compliance with correct formalities is assumed when a will is admitted to probate, but a will (or a provision of the will) will not be enforced when the testator is laboring under an insane delusion. Answer **C** is incorrect because there is no indication that anyone unduly influenced John. Answer **D** is incorrect. Although a testator may disinherit a child, the court will intervene to prevent an inequitable bequest when it is prompted by the testator's insane delusion. Although John may have the legal right to disinherit Clay, his insane delusion prevented him from executing a document that will be admitted to probate.

37. C Under UPC § 2-101(b), a decedent "by will may expressly exclude or limit the right of an individual or class to succeed to property of the decedent passing by intestate succession." "Will" is defined in § 1-201(56) to include "any testamentary instrument that merely . . . expressly excludes or limits the right of an individual or class to succeed to property of the decedent passing by intestate succession." So a document that does nothing more than disinherit an individual can nonetheless be a valid "will." The document here was entirely in the testator's handwriting, and was signed by him, so it meets the requirements for a holographic will. § 2-502(b). Therefore, it will be admitted to probate. Choice **A** is incorrect because the document is a valid will for the reasons just discussed. Choice **B** is legally incorrect (a natural father may disinherit his child). Choice **D** is incorrect because a mistake in the "inducement" to a will (*i.e.*, a mistake as to the surrounding facts or circumstances) will not be cause to refuse probate, unless the mistake is evident on the face of the will or is the product of an insane delusion; neither circumstance applies here.

38. A   When an attorney prepares a will in which he is a beneficiary and supervises its execution, the majority view is that a rebuttable presumption of undue influence arises. While there is no showing that Jones actually influenced Ellen, the facts that (1) the attorney-client relationship is a confidential one, and (2) the lawyer who prepared the will was employed by Jones, raise a presumption which must be rebutted. Choice **B** is incorrect. The question asks which argument is most likely to be successful. Because fraud must be proven by "clear and convincing" evidence, it is more difficult to establish than undue influence, which is presumed under these circumstances. Choice **C** is incorrect. There is no evidence that Ellen lacked testamentary capacity. Choice **D** is incorrect. A probate judge would not be likely to invalidate a will for this reason. He might refer Jones to the proper disciplinary authorities, but he would be more likely to use undue influence as the basis for rejecting the will.

39. B   Fraud occurs when the testator is willfully deceived as to facts which are material to his testamentary scheme, and these facts actually induce him to make, alter, or refrain from making, a testamentary gift. Robin had a duty to obtain a divorce before she remarried and Craig had a right to believe that Robin was in fact divorced. When she declared her marital status as single, she committed a fraud upon Craig. The fraud will only matter, for probate purposes, if the court concludes that the fraud "caused" the gift, *i.e.*, that the gift would not have been made had the fraud not been committed. Since the gift was made to Robin as "my wife," there is at least strong evidence that the gift was the product of Robin's fraud, so the court will probably conclude that the requisite causal connection between fraud and gift is established. The best remedy in light of Craig's dispositive language is to probate the will and impose a constructive trust upon Robin's share in favor of Aunt Martha. Otherwise, Robin's one-half would be distributed by intestacy. This would result in Craig's children taking part of his estate — a result which he obviously did not want. Answer **A** is incorrect. Although a true general statement, it does not provide for the effect of fraud by a beneficiary. Answers **C** and **D** are incorrect. Both would result in Aunt Martha's receiving nothing and in the distribution of Craig's entire estate to his children, a result Craig expressly did not want.

40. A   A general power of appointment is one which is exercisable in favor of the donee, his estate, his creditors, or the creditors of his estate. There are no limits on the persons to whom Ted can appoint, and so the power is a general one. Since there is no condition precedent, Ted is authorized to exercise the power during his lifetime by deed, and it is therefore "presently exercisable." Choice **B** is incorrect because Ted is not prohibited from appointing to himself, his estate, his creditors, or the creditors of his estate. Choice **C** is incorrect because Ted can exercise the power by deed during his life. Choice **D** is incorrect both (1) because Ted can appoint to himself, and (2) because Ted can exercise the power by deed.

41. C In order for a power of appointment to be deemed exercised by the will of the holder of the power, one of two things must be so: (1) the holder's will must manifest an intention to dispose of the property subject to the power; or (2) the power must be a general power and the creating instrument must not contain a gift if the power is not exercised. (UPC § 2-608). Because Ted's will did not refer at all to the power of appointment bestowed upon him in John's will, test (1) above is not satisfied. Further, Ted's power was a general power, ands John's will contained a gift to John's heirs if Ted failed to exercise the power. Therefore, test (2) isn't satisfied either. The residuary clause of Ted's will will probably not be construed as an exercise of the power. John's estate consequently passes to John's heirs. Choice **A** is incorrect; the residuary clause did not exercise Ted's power. Choices **B** and **D** are incorrect. The property subject to Ted's power passed to John's heirs by virtue of Ted's failure to exercise the power.

42. B The word "heirs" is usually taken to refer to those persons who, at the decedent's death, are entitled to succeed to the estate under the rules of intestate succession. UPC § 2-711. Art predeceased John and was not survived by issue. Thus, his share lapsed. Bob and Charles (John's "heirs") both survived John. Their shares *vested at John's death*, subject to being divested by Ted's exercise of the power over John's estate. Because Ted did not exercise the power, their shares passed by their wills to their wives. Choice **A** is incorrect because Art predeceased John. Art was not within the class of "heirs" at John's death. Choice **C** is incorrect, since (1) Bob's share vested prior to his death and Bob's wife was entitled to his share under his will, and (2) Charles' share passed to Marcy by will. Choice **D** is incorrect because the interests of Bob and Charles vested at John's death. They could dispose of their shares to their wives by will.

43. B When a general power of appointment is exercised, the property passes pursuant to the holder's instructions. Because the power was a general power and Ted exercised the appointive power in his will, the property became part of his overall testamentary scheme. Because (1) the appointed beneficiaries were dead, and (2) the anti-lapse statute is not applicable (the beneficiaries did not leave descendants), the property subject to Ted's power of appointment passes pursuant to Ted's residuary clause. Choice **A** is incorrect becuse the property subject to Ted's power was disposed of by him. Choices **C** and **D** are incorrect. John's estate passes under the residuary clause of Ted's will (not by intestacy).

44. C   If, after executing a will, the testator is divorced from the spouse who is a beneficiary under the will, the divorce revokes any disposition made by the will to the former spouse (UPC § 2-804(b)). The divorce automatically revoked the gift to Doris, and therefore, she will receive nothing. Choices **A**, **B** and **D** are all incorrect because Doris takes nothing from T's estate.

45. D   When a spouse marries the testator after the testator makes his will, the will is treated as a pre-marital will and the spouse is treated as an "omitted" spouse. Unless (1) it appears from the will that the will was made in contemplation of the marriage; or (2) the will expresses that it should be effective notwithstanding any subsequent marriage; or (3) the testator provided for the spouse outside the will and stated that the provision was in lieu of a testamentary provision -- the omitted spouse will receive her intestate share of that portion of the estate that the testator did not bequeath to his children from other, prior, marriages or relationships. (UPC § 2-301(a)). T's total estate was $130,000. After first deducting the specific bequest of $15,000 to Mike, Kay's share will be $100,000 plus 1/2 of the balance of $15,000, for a total of $107,500. The bequests to Ben will not be honored (see Answer 47 below). Choice **A** is mathematically incorrect. Choice **B** is incorrect both because it is mathematically incorrect and because the bequest to Ben will not be honored. Choice **C** is incorrect because Kay is an omitted spouse.

46. D   If one or more children of the testator were living when he executed his will and the will devised property to one or more of those children, then a pretermitted child would be entitled to a pro-rata share of the gifts to such child or children (UPC § 2-302(a)(2)). Because Liz was born after the will was executed, she is a pretermitted child and she will receive one-half of the $15,000 gift to Mike ($7,500). Choices **A** and **B** are mathematically incorrect under the required formula. Choice **C** is incorrect because Liz is a pretermitted child.

47. B   Any person who *kills* another *feloniously* and *intentionally* is not entitled to any benefit under the victim's will, and the decedent's estate passes as if the killer had disclaimed all provisions. (UPC § 2-803(c)). A person who commits *voluntary* manslaughter is deemed to have intended to kill or seriously injure the decedent (in contrast to a person who commits involuntary manslaughter). Therefore, Ben satisfies the "feloniously and intentionally kills" definition, and will receive nothing from T's estate. Choice **A** is incorrect. Even though the gift of Rex, Inc. stock may have been adeemed, Ben would still be entitled to the $1,000 general bequest. Choices **C** and **D** are incorrect because Ben receives nothing from T's estate.

48. **A** *Powers of appointment* are generally ***releasable***. Upon the release of a power of appointment, the property passes to previously designated takers in default; in this case, to Linda's living issue, per stirpes. Linda's release of the power was effective when delivered to Sam. Her attempt to exercise the power in her will was ineffective. The result is that the property held by Sam in trust passes to Linda's surviving issue, per stirpes. Choice **B** is incorrect because the attempted exercise of the power was ineffective. Choice **C** is incorrect because Martha is entitled to Karen's share. Choice **D** is incorrect because Ralph had provided for takers in default in the event the power was disclaimed or not exercised by Linda.

49. **C** A testamentary power may not be encumbered by or made subject to a contract with the holder of the power. Because contracts encumbering a ***testamentary*** power of appointment are unenforceable, Linda's exercise of the power is valid. Thus, Adam, Ron and Martha take equally. Choice **A** is incorrect because the contract between Linda and Adam is unenforceable. Adam may, of course, sue Linda's estate for restitution. Choice **D** is incorrect because Linda exercised the power through her will. Choice **B** is incorrect because Martha was specifically included among the appointees.

50. **C** A trust is created only if (1) the settlor has an intent to create a trust at the time, and (2) the settlor somehow manifests his intent to the outside world. The manifestation of intent may be by acts or statements that occur *after* the act creating the trust. *Rest. 2d of Trusts, § 24, Comment b.* In determining whether Alice intended the transfer to Jim to create a trust, statements made by Alice afterward (such as her statement to Jim two weeks later) would be considered by the court. In this case, they would probably be enough to establish Alice's intent to create a trust. (The issue would always be what Alice intended *at the time of the transfer;* an intent formed later would not count. Here, Alice's later statement shows that she probably always intended the transfer to Jim to be in trust.) Choices **A**, **B** and **D** are incorrect because they all assume that no valid trust was created. (If no valid trust was deemed created because Alice's statement was found to reflect only a post-transfer desire to invoke a trust, the correct answer would be choice **A**.)

51. B   When a trustor manifests an intent that a trust take effect at some *future point in time*, no trust is created. *Rest. 2d of Trusts*, § 26. Because Stephanie manifested an intent that the trust be created only upon her return from Europe, no valid trust was created. The farm was still part of her estate and passed to Rick pursuant to the will. Choice **A** is incorrect, because no trust was created by the letter to Sam. The letter expressed only an intent to create a trust in the future. Choice **C** is incorrect. Stephanie's death did not in itself have any testamentary effect. No trust was ever created because the letter to Sam manifested only the intent to create one in the future. Choice **D** is incorrect in that the farm passed pursuant to Stephanie's will, not by intestacy.

52. D   A special power is one which prevents the donee from appointing to himself, his estate, his creditors, or the creditors of his estate. Because Linda can appoint only to her issue, her power is a special (rather than a general) power. Because Linda is limited to appointment by will, the power is testamentary. Choice **A** is incorrect because Linda's power is neither general nor presently exercisable. The power cannot be exercised (1) in favor of Linda, her estate, her creditors, or the creditors of her estate, and (2) until her death. Choice **B** is incorrect in that the power cannot be exercised in favor of Linda, her estate, her creditors or the creditors of her estate. Choice **C** is incorrect in that the power can be exercised only by Linda's will.

53. D   A trust must *identify the beneficiaries* or provide a standard by which the beneficiaries can reasonably be ascertained. If the beneficiaries are indefinite, and there is no reasonable way to identify them, the trust fails. *Rest. 2d of Trusts, § 122.* The designation of "my three best friends" is probably an insufficient description of the beneficiaries, as evidenced by the fact that John, who was also Christina's friend, was unsure who her three best friends were. Thus, the trust probably fails, and Christina's entire estate passes to her mother. Choices **A** and **B** are incorrect because the trust failed. Choice **C** is incorrect. Christina never manifested any intent that Ann, Barbara and Cary should take anything outright.

54. B   A formal will must ordinarily be signed by the testator and at least two persons, each of whom witnessed either the signing of the will or the testator's acknowledgment of her signature or the will (UPC § 2-502). There is no requirement that the witnesses sign in front of each other. Because X and Y each signed after having witnessed T's execution of her will, T had a valid testamentary writing. Choice **A** is incorrect because the will was typed, and the "material provisions" were not in the testator's handwriting. Choice **C** is incorrect because there is no requirement under the UPC that the witnesses sign the will in each other's presence. Choice **D** is incorrect because there is no requirement that an attested will be dated to be valid.

55. **B**   Because T signed and acknowledged the will in the presence of X and Y, and they signed within a reasonable time thereafter, the writing is valid (UPC § 2-502). Choice **A** is incorrect because the will was typed, and the "material provisions" were not in the testator's handwriting. Choice **C** is incorrect because there is no requirement under the UPC that witnesses sign the will in the testator's presence. Choice **D** is incorrect because there is no requirement that witnesses actually read, or know the provisions of, the testator's will.

56. **C**   To be valid, a trust must have a named or ***ascertainable beneficiary*** capable of enforcing the trust. In most states, this beneficiary must be a ***human*** (or organization), not an animal. Although a few jurisdictions recognize honorary trusts (a trust with no definitely ascertainable human beneficiary and with only a specific non-charitable purpose), the majority do not. Trusts for the care of specific animals are honorary trusts. Under the majority view, the trust for Rusty's care will fail. (Note that the UPC has optional provisions, § 2-907(a) and (b), which validate a trust for a "designated domestic or pet animal." The trust is enforceable by a trustee designated in the trust instrument or one appointed by the court. In a jurisdiction with this provision in force, the correct answer would be Choice **A**.) Choice **A** is incorrect in most jurisdictions; there must be a named or reasonably identifiable ***individual*** who could enforce the trust. Choice **B** is incorrect because Bruce manifested no intent that Selma take the property in her own right. Choice **D** is incorrect because there is a right answer -- Choice **C**.

57. **C**   A condition in a trust unreasonably restraining marriage is usually not enforced. *Rest. 2d of Trusts, § 62, Comment h.* However, a gift over to an alternate beneficiary upon ***remarriage*** of the settlor's ***surviving spouse*** is usually not viewed as an unreasonable restraint upon marriage. *Id.* On the other hand, the condition imposed upon the children that they not marry is likely to be deemed unreasonable. This condition should be stricken, and the gift for their benefit should be without this restraint. *Rest. 2d, § 65.* The condition imposed upon Will that he not receive anything if he remarried is probably enforceable. Choice **A** is incorrect because the condition that Will forfeit his interest if he remarried is probably enforceable. Choice **B** is incorrect. The court is likely to find the condition imposed upon Will reasonable and enforceable. On the

other hand, the conditions imposed upon the children will be deemed unreasonable and will be stricken. Choice **D** is incorrect. If a condition is deemed invalid, it is stricken and the trust is otherwise enforced.

58. B   A secret trust arises when a will makes an outright gift in reliance upon the devisee's *oral promise* to hold the property as trustee for others. The agreement here is unenforceable as an express trust, because the oral agreement did not comply with the statutory formalities for wills (*e.g.*, the requirement that the terms be in writing). However, a *constructive trust* may be imposed in favor of the intended beneficiary to prevent the devisee's unjust enrichment, provided that the court is convinced by extrinsic evidence that the decedent relied on the devisee's promise to hold the property in trust for another. Here, Judith relied upon Earl's oral promise to hold the funds in trust for Grace. While Earl's promise is unenforceable as an express trust, it may be enforceable as a constructive trust to prevent Earl from being unjustly enriched. Choice **A** is incorrect in that a testamentary express trust cannot be created orally; it must be executed in accordance with the requisite formalities of a valid will. Choice **C** is incorrect; a resulting trust could not result because there was no *express* intention on the face of the will to create a trust. Choice **D** is incorrect; a majority of states would impose a constructive trust in this situation.

59. C   If a will disposes of property in trust, but fails to designate the beneficiary (sometimes called a semi-secret trust), the majority rule is that the property is held in a *resulting trust* for the residuary legatees of the trustor. Since Judith indicated in the will that the gift was made in trust, but failed to name the beneficiary in the will, the trust is a resulting one for the residuary legatees. A constructive trust will ordinarily not be imposed, because the will indicates on its face that Earl is taking the property as trustee and there's no opportunity for unjust enrichment by him. Choice **A** is incorrect. Grace will probably not be permitted to enforce the trust because she was not specifically named as beneficiary. Choice **B** is incorrect because a constructive trust will usually not be imposed where there is no opportunity for unjust enrichment by the trustee. Choice **D** is incorrect because Judith's will stated on its face that Earl was taking the bequest in trust.

60. A   A bank or savings account in the name of "X, in trust for Y" is called a "Totten trust," and is viewed as a type of informal will. Upon the death of X, the funds in a Totten account will be deemed to belong to Y. *See,* UPC § 6-212(b) and the Comment thereto; see also § 6-201(8)(ii). This construction will not apply where there is clear evidence that X did not intend a death benefit to Y, but there is no such evidence here. There-fore, Karen takes the funds in the account. Choice **B** is incorrect because there was a valid Totten trust. If no trust existed, Choice **B** would be the correct answer because Amy left all her property to Ed. Choices **C** and **D** are incorrect; even if no trust were found, the account would pass to Ed under the residuary clause of Amy's will.

61. C   A Totten trust is automatically revoked upon the death of the beneficiary prior to the death of the settlor. See UPC § 6-212(b)(2), last sentence. The contents of the account then belong to the settlor free of the trust. Therefore, the trust res passes to Ed under the terms of Amy's will. Choice **A** is incorrect in that the interest of Karen was divested when she predeceased Amy. Karen could not dispose of the account by her will. Choice **B** is incorrect because Karen's interest in the Totten trust was extinguished by her death before Amy. No one could take any interest in the account through Karen. Choice **D** is incorrect because Amy's will disposed of her estate to Ed.

62. D   The beneficial interest in a trust is ***alienable***, unless the trustor specifi-cally imposes some restraint upon alienation. Since no restraint upon the alienation of Carl's interest was stipulated in the trust, the assignment was valid. However, Carl could assign only his own equitable interest in the trust (*i.e.*, the trust continues in accordance with its terms). Choice **A** is incorrect; Carl's interest was alienable because the trustor did not spe-cifically restrain his right to alienate. Choice **B** is incorrect; both income and remainder interests are alienable. Choice **C** is incorrect; although Carl's interests may be assigned, the assignee can receive only an inter-est which is co-extensive with that enjoyed by Carl as the beneficiary-assignor.

63. A   In most jurisdictions, the first assignee in point of time prevails, regard-less of who first gives notice to the trustee. Because Carl's interest is an equitable one, he retained no interest which he could assign subse-quently. Choice **B** is incorrect; consideration is not a pertinent factor here (the bona fide purchaser rule is not applicable in this context). Choice **C** is incorrect as a statement of law (priority of ownership is ordinarily not based upon the order of notification to the trustee). Choice **D** is incorrect in that consideration is not pertinent on these facts.

64. C   The vested, equitable interest of a beneficiary in a trust can ordinarily be reached by a writ of execution against the beneficiary. However, only the debtor's interest can be levied upon. Lucille owns only a right to the income from the trust res. The trustee must, therefore, pay the income to the marshal (for application against the judgment) until (1) the judgment is satisfied, or (2) Lucille dies, whichever first occurs. Choice **A** is legally incorrect. In most states, a writ of execution will reach an equitable interest that is *not* contingent. Choices **B** and **D** are incorrect, because Lucille holds only a life interest. The courts will not usually order sale or conveyance of the entire property to satisfy a judgment against one who is solely a life tenant. Haskell, p. 226.

65. C   Despite the existence of a spendthrift clause, an income beneficiary may authorize payment of her income installments to another. However, the authorization may be revoked by the beneficiary at any time. The direction was valid, but revocable by Beatrix. The trustee may thus pay the income to Karen, until such time as Beatrix revokes the transfer. Choice **A** is incorrect because the assignment was valid (though revocable). Choice **B** is incorrect because it fails to state that the assignment is revocable. Choice **D** is incorrect. The transfer to Karen is not void and the debt to Karen is not satisfied until paid.

66. A   Under the majority rule, certain classes of creditors are not restrained by a spendthrift clause. The claims of a government entity for unpaid taxes are usually within this group. Choice **B** is incorrect; Beatrix' interest is only an income interest which does not enable the government or any one else to reach the trust principal. Choices **C** and **D** are incorrect because a spendthrift clause is *not* valid against a judgment by the U.S.

67. D   In the absence of words clearly expressing a trust intent, the court will rarely find such intent. John's will expressed only "the hope", instead of the mandate, that Ted would use the funds for his children. The court is unlikely to impose duties of trust on these facts. Words such as "hope", "wish" and "desire" are called precatory language; they are not usually enough to impose a trust. Choice **A** is incorrect because there are no mandatory words of trust intent. If, however, the court found that John did intend to create a trust, this would be the proper remedy. Choice **B** is incorrect; a resulting trust is usually imposed when the trust intent was expressed, but the trust purpose has failed. Choice **C** is incorrect; there is no equitable reason to impose a trust in favor of Bill.

68. B   The interest of a beneficiary which is subject to the discretion of the trustee may not be subjected to the claims of his creditors, until that discretion has been exercised. The creditor could levy upon Larry's remainder interest, because this interest is *not* subject to the trustee's discretion. However, a court would order that *no* amount be paid to the creditor until the last of Kathy's children died. Until that time, it would not be possible to determine Larry's *per capita* interest precisely. Choice **A** is incorrect. Larry's income interest is subject to the trustee's discretion (and therefore not attachable). Choice **C** is incorrect; it includes Larry's income interest, which is subject to the trustee's discretion and not subject to the creditor's claim. Choice **D** is incorrect because Larry's remainder interest may be attached by creditors, subject to the restriction discussed above.

69. C   A trustor cannot create a spendthrift trust in favor of himself. His interest is subject to the claims of creditors (present or prospective). Therefore, Ted may not create a spendthrift trust in favor of himself. Insofar as he retains an interest (*i.e.*, the income interest, in this case), it is subject to the claims of his creditors. Mae's, however, is not subject to the claims of Ted's creditors, unless the transfer constituted a fraud upon his creditors (*i.e.*, Ted was insolvent when the transfer of funds was ***initially*** made). Choices **A** and **B** are incorrect because Ted is not permitted to create a spendthrift trust in favor of himself. Choice **D** is incorrect because Mae's interest in the trust cannot be attached by Ted's creditors.

70. A   The purpose of a charitable trust must be to ***benefit either society as a whole*** or a substantial segment of the community. If a broad segment of society is benefitted, the purpose is usually approved even though the trust funds may be distributed to a limited number of recipients. Because (1) the purpose of her trust is to promote medical research leading to discovery of a cure for cancer, a worthy social purpose, and (2) the benefit of this accomplishment will be shared by a large segment of society, Leslie has probably created a valid charitable trust even though the beneficiaries are not presently ascertainable and may be very limited in number. Choice **B** is incorrect; because a large segment of society is benefitted, it is inconsequential that the recipients of the trust funds may be limited in number. Choices **C** and **D** are incorrect; charitable trusts are exempt from the Rule Against Perpetuities.

71. D   Courts have enforced trusts "for charitable purposes" even though the trustee was authorized to select any charitable purpose. The trustee can probably use the money for any purpose which comes within the definition of "charitable" as that term is defined under the applicable law. Choice **A** is incorrect because the beneficiaries are ascertainable by reason of the trustee's decisions; the trustee can select any group of beneficiaries which is charitable in character. Choice **B** is incorrect because charitable trusts are exempt from the Rule Against Perpetuities. Choice **C** is incorrect; the trustee is not limited in his choices but may utilize the trust res for any charitable purpose.

72. D   When the purpose of a trust is to encourage illegal activity, the trust is invalid. A trust created for the purpose of rewarding persons who have broken the law is invalid. Many people believe with Lynn that the drug laws are too punitive and restrictive. But they may not commit their funds to encourage violation of the law as long as it remains the law. It would be proper for Lynn to campaign politically to change the law, but not to reward violators of the law. The trust will fail and the trust res will pass to Max under intestacy principles. Choices **A** and **B** are incorrect because the primary purpose of the trust is to reward persons who have broken the law. Choice **C** is incorrect; there is no presently cognizable general charitable purpose for this trust. The only persons receiving a benefit are those who have engaged in activity which is defined as illegal.

73. D   A charitable trust cannot benefit a profit-making organization. Although International University is an educational institution, it is described as a profit-making organization. It is, therefore, disqualified as a valid charitable beneficiary. Choice **A** is incorrect; even though the purpose of the trust is education, it may not benefit a profit-making organization. Choice **B** is incorrect; the trust fails because the beneficiary of the trust is a profit-making entity. Choice **C** is incorrect; although the students may be indigent, the beneficiary is a profit-making organization.

74. B   When the particular charitable purpose specified by a trustor has become impossible, or impracticable to accomplish, and it is determined that the trustor had a general charitable intent, a court may modify the trust so as to carry out the trustor's purpose to the extent that it is possible to do so. The theory permitting such modification is called the *"cy pres"* doctrine. Although Terry's alma mater was chosen as the recipient of the gift, it may be argued that Terry's primary purpose was to benefit "worthy students from Arizona." Thus, the cy pres doctrine should be used to allow the gift to be given to another charitable institution whose primary purpose is education and whose students include students from Arizona. Choice **A** is incorrect in that a charitable gift cannot be made to a profit-making organization. Choice **C** is correct only if the charitable gift is held to fail. In this instance, the broader purpose of educating Arizona students can be carried out without destroying the trust. Choice **D** is incorrect; if the trust failed, the money would pass to Terry's parents.

75. C   Where the particular charitable purpose specified by a settlor has become impossible or impracticable to accomplish, and it is determined that the trustor had a general charitable intent, the court may modify the trust so as to carry out the trustor's purpose to the extent that it is possible to do so. On these facts, the court will probably sustain the trust but remove any racial restrictions. If, however, it decides to retain the provisions limiting the scholarships to male students who are not atheists, its decision will probably be affirmed on appeal even against an argument of sexual and religious discrimination. There is a strong policy in favor of sustaining charitable gifts wherever possible. Choice **A** is incorrect because Settlor expressed strong feelings against using the funds for the education of atheists. It would therefore be inconsistent with his charitable intent to repudiate this constraint. Choice **B** is incorrect; the racial restrictions would not be permitted to any institution. Choice **D** is incorrect in that the trust can be enforced with modifications which are consistent with the trustor's overall charitable intent.

76. B A trustee is ordinarily prohibited from any type of self-dealing, which constitutes a breach of fiduciary duty. The trustee cannot personally purchase trust property even for its fair market value. *Rest. 2d. of Trusts, § 170, and Comment b.* Although Edward had an implied right to sell the trust asset, the sale of trust property *to himself* was prohibited. Choice **A** is incorrect; Edward did have an implied power to sell trust assets under these circumstances. Choice **C** is incorrect; Edward breached his fiduciary duties by self-dealing, even if he paid fair market value. Choice **D** is incorrect; self-dealing is prohibited to a fiduciary.

77. A A trustee has no implied power to ***borrow funds*** or to encumber trust property. A trustee cannot ordinarily borrow funds against trust assets or against the general credit of the trust, unless he has been specifically granted that power. Choice **B** is incorrect. Edward violated his duty whether or not the net income was reduced. Choice **C** is incorrect; a trustee has no implied power to borrow funds against trust property. He must have the express authority to borrow. Choice **D** is legally incorrect (Edward did breach his fiduciary duty by exercising a power which he did not possess).

78. C A trustee must act within the bounds of reasonable judgment in carrying out the purpose of the trust. *Rest. 2d of Trusts, § 187.* The grant of sole, absolute or uncontrolled discretion does not completely insulate the trustee from judicial review. Even though "sole, absolute and uncontrolled" discretion was granted to the trustee, she was required to carry out the purpose of the trust in a good faith, non-arbitrary manner. The favoring of one beneficiary over another without reason would be arbitrary, and an abuse of discretion, for which the court could impose liability. Choices **A** and **B** are incorrect in that the court does have the power to review the decisions of the trustee in these circumstances (*i.e.*, making income payments only to the oldest child, who might be the least needy); and there is no presumption that the trustee has acted reasonably when the facts (preferring one child to the others) would support a contrary presumption. Choice **D** is incorrect in that the court is not permitted to substitute its own judgment, but may impose liability for actions that are so unreasonable as to amount to an abuse of discretion by the trustee.

79. D   Because real property values historically fluctuate greatly, a trustee is generally not authorized to invest in ***unimproved land*** for resale or appreciation. However, a trust instrument may specifically authorize the trustee to make such an investment. Here, Ted had no such authority. Choice **A** is incorrect; although a trustee is governed by the prudent investor rule, investment in unimproved land for appreciation or resale is deemed imprudent by its very nature. Choice **B** is incorrect in that the applicable rule is not mitigated by an appraisal which happens to support the trustee's judgment. Choice **C** is incorrect; an otherwise improper investment may be specifically authorized by the trust instrument.

80. C   Co-trustees exercise their trust powers jointly, and the exercise normally requires unanimity. *Rest. 2d of Trusts, § 194.* If there is an emergency, the requirement of unanimity can be dispensed with; however, the taking of an appeal on these facts is not likely to be construed as such an emergency. Able could seek a court order dispensing with the need for Baker's consent and cooperation in the appeal. But without the order, Able can't simply act on his own. Choice **A** is incorrect because Able may not appeal the judgment unilaterally. If he proceeds with the appeal anyway in good faith, he may be entitled to reimbursement for the costs. Choice **B** is incorrect because of the requirement of unanimity. Choice **D** is incorrect. So long as Baker acts with reasonable business judgment and in good faith, he may refuse to join in the appeal.

81. D   A trustee must ***personally administer*** the powers of the trust. While Karl is allowed to employ persons to advise him in the exercise of his powers, he cannot delegate administration or control of the trust to others or disavow his own duty to exercise a trustee's powers. Choice **A** is incorrect in that Karl cannot completely, even temporarily, relieve himself of his duties as trustee. Karl will remain liable for breach of his duties. Choice **B** is incorrect in that the powers of the trustee simply cannot be delegated. Edward may assist Karl in performing Karl's trust duties but he may not assume or exercise them. Choice **C** is incorrect in that Karl may not delegate to Edward even those powere which might be considered discretionary.

82. B A trustee may employ agents to perform services for the trust, so long as the trustee exercises the care of a reasonably prudent person in selecting the agents and continues to oversee the performance of their assigned services. The duty to make investment decisions is not ***totally*** delegable. Karl was required to inquire of Edward his reasons for investing in particular stocks and the likelihood of their financial success. After these inquiries, Karl was required to make the investment decision himself. If Karl failed in either duty, he will be strictly liable for any loss (even if a reasonably prudent investor might have made the same investment decision as Edward). Choice **A** is incorrect; Karl is liable even if the stock would have been purchased by the prudent investor. Choice **C** is incorrect in that Karl was obliged to oversee, inquire into and approve Edward's decisions. Choice **D** is incorrect; even if Karl exercised reasonable care in selecting Edward, he was still obliged to "supervise" and review all of Edward's investment recommendations.

83. B It is a breach of a trustee's fiduciary duty to borrow funds from the trust for his personal use. *Rest. 2d of Trusts, § 170, Comment l.* In addition to repaying the principal and interest of the loan, Karl must forfeit all profits which he made as a consequence of his loans from the trust. *Rest. 2d of Trusts, § 206, Illustration 8.* Choice **A** is incorrect; Karl is legally obliged to remit any profits to the trust. It's immaterial to the central issue of trust that no damage occurred. Choices **C** and **D**. It's plain and simple -- Karl has breached his fiduciary duty to the trust. It was improper for him to borrow funds from the trust under any circumstances and is liable whether or not the trust suffered any losses and whether or not he repaid his loans.

84. D An exculpatory clause in a trust is sufficient to excuse ordinary negligence; as a matter of public policy, however, it is not ordinarily construed as relieving a trustee of ***gross*** negligence. The exculpatory clause here would therefore be sufficient to excuse Amy from liability based upon ordinary negligence, but not gross negligence. Choice **A** is incorrect in that Amy would be liable for the consequences of her gross negligence -- *e.g.*, if she had invested in the new business without conducting any investigation at all. Choice **B** is incorrect in that if Amy were liable at all, the loss of income resulting from her negligence might affect the other beneficiaries of the trust as well as Amy herself (Amy was entitled only to that portion of income necessary for her own support, maintenance and education). Choice **C** is incorrect; if Amy's omission constituted gross negligence, she would be liable to the other beneficiaries for lost principal.

85. A   A trustee is ordinarily ***personally liable*** for breach of a contract regarding trust assets. A trustee held liable for breach of contract has a right of indemnification from the trust, so long as she acted in good faith. While Laura is personally liable as trustee, she has a right of indemnification from the trust, assuming she acted in good faith. We are dealing here with an *inter vivos* trust. If this had been a *testamentary* trust governed by the UPC, the result would be different: UPC § 7-306(a) says that, unless otherwise provided in the contract, a trustee is not personally liable on contracts properly entered into in his fiduciary capacity in the course of administration of the trust estate, unless he fails to reveal his representative capacity and identify the trust estate in the contract. Here, Laura signed the contract as trustee. Choice **B** is incorrect; Laura is personally liable for the breach. Choice **C** is incorrect; Laura probably has a right to indemnification because she appears to have acted in good faith. Choice **D** is incorrect; Laura has a right of indemnification whether or not the trust document contains an exculpatory clause.

86. C   A trustee is ordinarily personally liable for all torts which he commits during his administration of the trust, whether or not he is personally at fault. (But if this were a *testamentary* trust governed by the UPC, the rule would be different: UPC § 7-306(b) provides that a trustee is personally liable for torts committed in the course of administering the trust estate only if he is personally at fault.) Furthermore, a trustee cannot obtain ***indemnity*** from the trust when he was personally at fault. Because Bill was personally at fault (*i.e.*, he was driving negligently), he may *not* receive indemnity from the trust estate. The fact that Bill was arguably acting in the course of administering the trust is irrelevant. Choice **A** is incorrect in that Bill may not indemnify himself under these circumstances. Choice **B** is incorrect in that Bill is personally liable. Choice **D** is incorrect. An exculpatory clause ordinarily insulates a trustee from responsibility to reimburse a trust for diminishing its assets by his errors in judgment. It does not authorize indemnity for the personal negligence of the trustee in causing injury to third parties. (It should be mentioned that the trust assets are ordinarily not available to pay claims for torts personally committed by the trustee in the course of administering the trust. Even if Bill is judgment-proof, Phyllis will probably not be able to recover against the trust's assets.)

87. B A trustee is personally liable for all torts committed by employees of the trust while acting within the scope of their employment. He is, in fact and in law, the employer. (Again, note that in the case of a *testamentary* trust, UPC § 7-306(b) provides that a trustee is personally liable for torts committed in the course of administration of the trust estate only if he is personally at fault.) A trustee is ordinarily entitled to indemnity if he was not personally at fault. Bill is personally liable under the doctrine of *respondeat superior*; but since he was not personally at fault he may seek indemnity from trust property. However, Bill's recovery is limited to the trust assets; he cannot seek indemnity from the beneficiaries themselves. In this case, he must personally pay the excess damages ($100,000). Choice **A** is incorrect; a trustee may *not* ordinarily seek indemnity from the beneficiaries individually. Choices **C** and **D** are both incorrect in at least one respect -- Bill is personally liable.

88. A In most states, *stock dividends* are always treated as principal, and thus allocated to the *corpus* of a trust. Choices **B**, **C** and **D** are all incorrect because stock dividends are usually allocated exclusively and entirely to the corpus of a trust.

89. C When there is an income interest in a trust separate from the principal interest, the trustee is generally obligated to *sell unproductive property*. *Rest. 2d of Trusts, § 240*. (This rule also applies to "under-productive" assets, *i.e.*, those which produce so little current income, compared with what could be earned from an alternative investment having the same principal value, that it's unfair to the income beneficiary to keep the low-income assets.) All proceeds from the sale of such property must be added to the corpus of the trust. Choices **A** and **B** are incorrect in that Taft is obliged to sell unproductive property. Choice **D** is incorrect; all proceeds from the sale of unproductive trust property are allocated to the corpus. The monies would then be invested in an income- producing asset, thereby benefitting both the income interests and the principal interests.

90. D Under the majority rule, *maintenance, taxes* and *insurance* pertaining to trust assets are paid, in the first instance, *from income* (even though these expenditures protect both income and remainder interests). Under the majority view, all three expenditures are charged to the income beneficiaries. Choice **A** is incorrect in that taxes and insurance are also charged against trust income. Choice **B** is incorrect in that insurance is also charged against trust income. Choice **C** is incorrect in that the maintenance of trust assets is also charged against income.

91. D   In most states, a settlor does not retain the power to ***modify or revoke*** an *inter vivos* trust. These powers must be ***expressly retained*** at the time the trust is created. *Rest. 2d of Trusts, §§ 330, 331*. Because the facts indicate that Ellen did not expressly retain a power to modify or revoke, she can do neither. Choices **A**, **B** and **C** are incorrect because Ellen did not explicitly retain the power to modify or revoke the trust.

Table of References to the Uniform Probate Code (UPC)

Table of References to the Restatement (2d) of Trusts

Index

References are to the number of the question raising the issue.
"E" indicates an Essay Question; "M" indicates a Multiple-Choice Question